IS SOMEONE ON THE MOON?

KEN HUDNALL
OMEA PRESS
EL PASO, TEXAS 79912

2   IS SOMEONE ON THE MOON?

IS SOMEONE ON THE MOON?

COPYRIGHT © 2018 KEN HUDNALL

All rights reserved. No part of the book may be reproduced or transmitted in any form or by any means, graphic, electronic, or mechanical, including photocopying, recording, taping or by any information storage or retrieval system, without the permission in writing of the author.

OMEGA PRESS

http://www.kenhudnall.com

FIRST EDITION

Printed in the United States of America

OTHER WORKS BY THE SAME AUTHOR UNDER THE NAME KEN HUDNALL FROM OMEGA PRESS

MANHATTAN CONSPIRACY SERIES
Blood on the Apple
Capitol Crimes
Angel of Death
Confrontation

THE OCCULT CONNECTION
UFOs, Secret Societies and Ancient Gods
The Hidden Race
Flying Saucers
UFOs and the Supernatural
UFOs and Secret Societies
UFOs and Ancient Gods
Evidence of Alien Contact
Intervention
Secrets of Dulce
Unidentified Flying Objects
Sensual Alien Encounters
Strange Creatures From Time and Space
Beyond Roswell
Alien Encounters
Mysteries of Space
Battle of Los Angeles

DARKNESS
When Darkness Falls
Fear the Darkness

SPIRITS OF THE BORDER
(with Connie Wang)
The History and Mystery of El Paso Del Norte
The History and Mystery of fort Bliss, Texas

(with Sharon Hudnall)
The History and Mystery of the Rio Grande
The History and Mystery of New Mexico
The History and Mystery of the Lone Star State
The History and Mystery of Arizona
The History and Mystery of Tombstone, AZ
The History and Mystery of Colorado
Echoes of the Past
El Paso: A City of Secrets
Tales From the Nightshift
The History and Mystery of Sin City
The History and Mystery of Concordia
The History and Mystery of ASARCO
Military Ghosts
School Spirits
Restless spirits
Railroad Ghosts
Nautical Ghosts
Haunted Hotels
Haunted Hotels in Arizona and Colorado
Ghosts of Albuquerque
The History and Mystery of Tucson
The History and Mystery of Santa Fe

SHADOW WARS
The Shadow Rulers
The Secret Elite

THE ESTATE SALE MURDERS
Dead Man's Diary
A Bloody Afternoon of Fun

BOOK OF SECRETS
Ancient Secrets
Secrets of the Dark Web

Northwood Conspiracy

No Safe Haven: Homeland Insecurity

Where No Car Has Gone Before

Seventy Years and No Losses: The History of the Sun Bowl

How Not To Get Published

Lost Cities and Hidden Tunnels Along the Border

Vampires, Werewolves and Things That Go Bump in The Night

Border Escapades of Billy the Kid

Criminal law for the Layman

Understanding Business Law

Language of the Law

Death of Innocence: The Life and Death of Vince Foster

The Veterans' Practice Primer

Why Would They Say It?

PUBLISHED BY PAJA BOOKS
The Occult Connection: Unidentified Flying Objects

PUBLISHED BY PRUNE DANISH PRESS
Why Would They Say It?

DEDICATION

As with all of my endeavors, this would not be possible without the support and assistance of my lovely wife, Sharon Hudnall.

TABLE OF CONTENTS

CHAPTER ONE 11
WE WENT TO THE MOON 11
CHAPTER TWO 19
EXTRA-TERRESTRIAL EXPOSURE LAW 19
CHAPTER THREE 29
WHAT DID WE HAVE TO FEAR? 29
CHAPTER FOUR 37
SUPPORT FOR THE EXISTENCE OF UFOS AND ALIEN VISITORS 37
CHAPTER FIVE 51
FACTS ABOUT THE MOON 51
CHAPTER SIX 65
STRANGE ACTIVITY ON THE MOON 65
CHAPTER SEVEN 73
BEHIND THE SCENES 73
CHAPTER EIGHT 81
WHAT CAUSED SUSPICION THAT MIGHT BE LIFE ON THE MOON? 81
CHAPTER NINE 93
A FINAL POSSIBILITY 93
APPENDIX A 99
CHRONOLOGICAL CATALOG OF REPORTED LUNAR EVENTS 99
APPENDIX B 187
OPERATION HORIZON 187

INDEX 207

CHAPTER ONE
WE WENT TO THE MOON

Figure 1: The Columbia, the command module of Apollo 11.

Though many still seem to doubt it, there is little question that astronauts from the United States of America landed on the Moon. The NASA mission known as Apollo 11 was the fifth manned mission in NASA's Apollo Program. It was Apollo 11's mission commander Neil Armstrong and pilot Buzz Aldrin that were the first known humans to walk on the Moon.

Figure 2: This is the Eagle, the lunar module that landed on the moon.

Though not often mentioned, while Armstrong and Aldrin enjoyed their lunar stroll, astronaut Michael Collins remained in the command capsule in orbit around the Moon. The lunar module containing Armstrong and Aldrin, known to the world as Eagle landed on the surface of the Moon in an internationally televised event on July 20, 1969. The time of this historic event was 20:17 UTC[1].

---

[1] It should also be noted that the first known landing of an earth launched vehicle was by the Soviets with their unpowered hard landing of LUNA 2 in 1959. LUNA 1 tried for a hard landing on the Moon earlier in 1959 but failed. The United States was not able to successfully make a hard landing on the Moon until 1962.

There was a lot of political concerns surrounding the race to be the first country to successfully land men on the moon and get them safely home. The United States and the Soviet Union, firm allies during World War II had become adversaries and were stock piling weapons for what many believed would be a very violent World War III. Once both sides had the hydrogen bomb, there seemed little chance that there would be a lasting peace on the planet. Both sides seemed intent on proving who had the best and strongest military. This naturally led to faceoffs between opposing troops in various locations around the globe.

Figure 3:Crew of the Apollo 11, Michael Collins, Buzz Aldrin and Neil Armstrong.

To make matter worse, heretofore little-known scientific principles were being thoroughly investigated in the wake of the scientific marvels discovered by victorious troops from both sides in the captured research facilities of the Third Reich and as off shoots of the research that led to the American atom bomb.

It seemed only natural the this formerly military research should be turned to the question of whether or not mankind could leave this planet and colonize the stars. Just

Figure 4: Buzz Aldrin salutes the American flag in the vacuum on the Moon.

as the belief that whoever controlled the planet would control space, so too, it proved true that whoever controlled space, controlled the planet as well. In fact, in the 1960s, an unbelievable amount of resources of both the United States and the Soviet Union, the world's two super powers, were committed to what came to be known as the space race. The question seemed to be would he East or the West control the solar system. Pragmatically and politically, it seemed to many this was a better use of these resources than the ever-present arms race. But perhaps there was a most important reason for the space race than mere competitiveness.

THE ROSWELL INCIDENT

In July of 1947, the much-discussed crash of an unidentified flying object (UFO) took place near Roswell, New Mexico. Now the question of whether or not there were space aliens in the solar system or perhaps on the planet became one of concern to both governments. This gave rise to numerous conspiracy theories and discoveries of crashed UFOs by both military as well as non-military personnel that were hastily hidden by governments on both side of the world for fear of the public panicking on a large scale.

Research has shown that there have been a number of contacts between the occupants of UFOs and humans as well as crashes of said craft on the earth. Clearly contact between the occupants of the UFOs and humans could easily become a matter of national security. Hence, a program of suppressing all such reports became a topic priority.

It is also fascinating to find that at the very same time that our government told us that there were no aliens and that every UFO sighting was either a hoax, a misidentification of some common item or just an outright lie or a figment of the imagination of the witness, there was in existence a federal law-making contact with said imaginary occupants of these non-existent UFOs a federal crime. So, the question becomes, what did we expect to find on the moon?

CHAPTER TWO

EXTRA-TERRESTRIAL EXPOSURE LAW

Since the time of the Roswell UFO crash in 1947, the government has gone to great lengths to deny even the possibility that there are UFOs or aliens visiting the earth. So, it is with some puzzlement that we submit the contents of a federal law that was passed in 1969.

It takes a great deal in the way of time and money to pass a federal law, not to mention the necessity of creating a mechanism to enforce said law. So why was it that at the same time numerous federal agencies were screaming to the heavens that there were no UFOs or aliens or anything else strange would the federal government go to the trouble of creating and passing a federal law, making contract with said non-existent entities a federal crime? This simply defies logic.

From its terms, anyone found guilty of such illegal contact with the imaginary UFOs or non-extent aliens would face imprisonment for up to one year as well as a fine of $5,000.00 Such exposure would also result in being quarantined under armed guard by the NASA Administrator without a hearing of any type.

Now clearly the law was passed to protect the earth from possible biological contamination resulting from the US Apollo Space Program and other space exploration programs. Clearly the US Government was concerned that contact with extraterrestrial bacteria could result in a worldwide plague.

Title 14, Section 1211 of U.S. Federal Code: Forbidding Contact With Extraterrestrials

1211.100 Title 14 - Aeronautics and Space

Part 1211 - Extra-terrestrial Exposure

1211.100 - Scope

This part establishes: (a) NASA policy, responsibility and authority to guard the Earth against any harmful contamination or adverse changes in its environment resulting from personnel, spacecraft and other property returning to the Earth after landing on or coming within the atmospheric envelope of a celestial body; and (b) security requirements, restrictions and safeguards that are necessary in the interest of national security.

1211.101 - Applicability

The provisions of this part to all NASA manned and unmanned space missions which land or come within the atmospheric envelope of a celestial body and return to the Earth.

1211.102 - Definitions

(a) "NASA" and the "Administrator" mean, respectively the National Aeronautics and Space Administration and the administrator of the National Aeronautics and Space Administration or his authorized representative.

(b) "Extra-terrestrially exposed" means the state of condition of any person, property, animal or other form of life or matter whatever, who or which has:

(1) Touched directly or come within the atmospheric envelope or any other celestial body; or

(2) Touched directly or been in close proximity to (or been exposed indirectly to) any person, property, animal or other form of life or matter who or which has been extra-terrestrially exposed by virtue of paragraph (b)(1) of this section.

For example, if person or thing "A" touches the surface of the Moon, and on "A's" return to Earth, "B" touches "A" and, subsequently, "C" touches "B", all of these - "A" through "C" inclusive - would be extra-terrestrially exposed ("A" and "B" directly; "C" indirectly).

(c) "Quarantine" means the detention, examination and decontamination of any persons, property, animal or other form of life or matter whatever that is extra-terrestrially exposed, and includes the apprehension or seizure of such person, property, animal or other form of life or matter whatever.

(d) "Quarantine period" means a period of consecutive calendar days as may be established in accordance with 1211.104 (a).

(a) Administrative actions. The Administrator or his designee shall in his discretion:

(1) Determine the beginning and duration of a quarantine period with respect to any space mission; the quarantine period as it applies to various life forms will be announced.

(2) Designate in writing quarantine officers to exercise quarantine authority.

(3) Determine that a particular person, property, animal, or other form of life or matter whatever is extra- terrestrially exposed and quarantine such person, property, animal, or other form of life or matter whatever. The quarantine may be based only on a determination, with or without the benefit of a hearing, that there is probable cause to believe that such person, property, animal or other form of life or matter whatever is extra- terrestrially exposed.

(4) Determine within the United States or within vessels or vehicles of the United States the place, boundaries, and rules of operation of necessary quarantine stations.

(5) Provide for guard services by contract or otherwise, as many be necessary, to maintain security and inviolability of quarantine stations and quarantined persons, property, animals or other form of life or matter whatever.

(6) Provide for the subsistence, health and welfare of persons quarantined under the provisions of this part.

(7) Hold such hearings at such times, in such manner and for such purposes as may be desirable or necessary under this part, including hearings for the purpose of creating a record for use in making any determination under this part for the purpose of reviewing any such determination.

(b) (3) During any period of announced quarantine, no person shall enter or depart from the limits of the quarantine station without permission of the cognizant NASA officer. During such period, the posted perimeter of a quarantine station shall be secured by armed guard.

(b) (4) Any person who enters the limits of any quarantine station during the quarantine period shall be deemed to have consented to the quarantine of his person if it is determined that he is or has become extra-terrestrially exposed.

(b) (5) At the earliest practicable time, each person who is quarantined by NASA shall be given a reasonable opportunity to communicate by telephone with legal counsel or other persons of his choice.

1211.107 Court or other process

(a) NASA officers and employees are prohibited from discharging from the limits of a quarantine station any quarantined person, property, animal or other form of life or matter whatever during order or other request, order or demand an announced quarantine period in compliance with a subpoena, show cause or any court or other authority without the prior approval of the General Counsel and the Administrator.

(b) Where approval to discharge a quarantined person, property, animal or other form of life or matter whatever in compliance with such a request, order or demand of any court or other authority is not given, the person to whom it is directed shall, if possible, appear in court or before the other authority and respectfully state his inability to comply, relying for his action on this 1211.107.

1211.108 Violations

Whoever willfully violates, attempts to violate, or conspires to violate any provision of this part or any regulation or order issued under this part or who enters or departs from the limits of a quarantine station in disregard of the quarantine rules or regulations or without permission of the NASA quarantine officer shall be fined not more

than $5,000 or imprisoned not more than 1 year, or both.

This law was enacted on July 16, 1969 shortly before our moon landing later in July of 1968. Now as I pointed out in **THE OCCULT CONNECTION: UFOS, SECRET SOCIETIES AND ANCIENT GODS**[2], by the terms of this law, anyone who simply comes in contact with either a space alien or a UFO is automatically designated as a wanted felon. He or she does not get a trial nor a hearing of any kind. This certainly tends to support the premise that the government knew that it was possible to come into contact with a UFO or an alien, otherwise why pass this unusual law.

Now you might believe that it would take a hearing to prove whether or not the offender actually came in contact with the UFO or the alien, but according to the terms of the law, if the NASA Administrator said that he or she believed

---

[2] Hudnall, Ken, THE OCCULT CONNECTION: UFOS, SECRET SOCIEITIES AND ANCIENT GODS, The Omega Foundation, Anaheim, California, March 1990.

that the offender had come in contact with the UFO or the alien, then as a matter of law, the accused had come into contact with these proscribed UFOs or aliens and immediate incarceration was automatic. The right of Habeas Corpus was specifically denied under the terms of this law in direct contravention to the rights and privileges guaranteed to US citizens under the U.S. Constitution.

Now the reader might believe that under the provisions of Section 1211.101 APPLICABILITY that the law applied only to NASA manned and unmanned space missions, however, according to George Andrews in his book EXTRA-TERRISTRAILS AMONG US[3], the question about the applicability of this law was put to NASA's general counsel, S. Neil Hosenball[4]. According to Mr. Hosenball, the law was most definitely applicable to space

---

[3] Andrews, George, EXTRA-TERRESTRIALS AMONG US, Llewellyn Publications, St. Paul, Minnesota, 55164-0383
[4] 1925 – 2009. He served as NASA's general counsel from 1975 – 1985.

vehicles and extra-terrestrial personnel not origination on this earth.

As if this is not strange enough, the law was rescinded on Friday, April 26, 1991 by the Administrator of NASA, Richard H. Truly since the law had *served its purpose and is no longer in keeping with current policy.* This would tend to make the author curious about what was the law's purpose and what is the current policy?

CHAPTER THREE
WHAT DID WE HAVE TO FEAR?

So, it was that in mid 1969, the U.S. Government passed a federal law[5] making it a crime to come into contact with a UFO or an alien. Of course, at the same time, this same government was stating firmly that there were no UFOs or aliens.

While the author was stationed in the Panama Canal Zone in the 1970s, he was aware of a number of sightings that were reported by soldiers within the 193rd Infantry Brigade. In each case, field grade officers threatened the

---

[5] USC Title 14, Section 1211.

reporter with severe penalties if they spoke of what they had seen to anyone else.

There were some who were of the strong belief that there was a base for these craft somewhere in the jungle south of the Panama Canal Zone, but we were forbidden to enter the area in question. As I became friends with some of the Panamanians worked on the post, I heard stories of strange things seen in the jungle and of certain areas that even the locals refused to enter. However, when this author tried to enter those area with his unit during individual training, he was prohibited to the point of being threatened with court martial.

So, what do (or did) we have to fear from exploring the question of whether or not there were UFOs or aliens? To try and answer this question, we need to go back to what has become known as the ROSWELL Incident. For those unfamiliar with this matter it was alleged that in July of 1947, a UFO crashed outside of Roswell, New Mexico.

There have been a number of good books published that explored this matter in detail. Of course, to be perfectly truthful, the crash was actually closer to the small community of Corona, New Mexico. However, when word of this matter reached the closest military post, it was Roswell Army Airfield in Roswell, New Mexico, hence it became known as the Roswell crash.

Stationed at Roswell Army Airfield at the time was the 509th Bomber Group which was one of the few units trained in the use of nuclear weapons. Once receiving the report from the sheriff, the commander of the 509th, Colonel William Blanchard dispatched his G2 (Intelligence Officer) Major Jesse Marcel to investigate the report.

According to Major Marcell, he found a debris field that stretched for some distance. According to reports he filled the back of a military sedan with many pieces of this material which his son, Jesse Marcell, Jr. later discussed.

Major Marcel was firm in his belief that the debris was not from an earthly craft.

Initially, the 509th ordered the RAAFB Public Information Officer (PIO), Lieutenant Walter Haut, to issue a formal press release that the Army[6] had captured a Flying Saucer, which was later rescinded on orders from higher headquarters. In fact, General Roger M. Ramey went to great lengths to discredit the findings of the 509th to the point of faking several photos showing that what the 509th identified as a flying saucer was actually a weather balloon. So why the secrecy?

As intended, the Roswell story died out as the military did everything in its power to discredit the report and the witnesses. This also included Counter Intelligence Group (CIG) and military police officers threatening those who did or may have seen something they should not have.

---

[6] It was until later in 1947 that the United States Air Force was created so at this point in 1947 it was still the Army Air Corp.

Some witnesses who were working on the local ranches who were from Mexico as a result of the official threats returned to their country vowing never to return.

Unfortunately for the military, refusing to admit that they existed did nothing to stop the UFOs from flying or the occupants of said craft from wandering around the countryside. The periodic stories became an avalanche after the Soviet Union's successful launch of Sputnik 1 in October 1957. In fact, from a classified FBI report dated November 12, 1957 that was released under a Freedom of Information Request (FOIA), it was reported that for the prior two weeks there had been numerous reports of UFOs sightings as well as reports of alien and human contacts.

All the while ridiculing the very idea of UFOs or aliens, the highest levels of our government were very concerned about the discovery that there were others in the universe besides ourselves would do to society as a whole. It may have been with this ominous issue in mind that the

National Aeronautics and Space Administration (NASA) was created on July 29, 1958 as an independent agency of the executive branch of the federal government[7].

In the early 1960s, Donald N. Michael, of the Brookings Institution prepared a study on behalf of NASA's Committee on Long Range Studies that was entitled: ***Proposed Studies on the Implications of Peaceful Space Activities for Human Affairs***. The question proposed by this study is very simple. What would be the reaction of society if it were found that there were really aliens?

The big issue that surfaced on page 183 of this report referenced that fact that "***Anthropological filed contain many examples of societies, sure of their place in the universe, which have disintegrated when they have had to associate with previously unfamiliar societies espousing different ideas and different life ways; others that have***

---

[7] Interestingly, while NASA is usually called the civilian space agency, its charter makes it clear that NASA is a part of the Department of Defense.

survived such an experience did so by paying the price of changes in values and attitudes and behavior."

In other words, the very knowledge that there were advanced creatures out there could have a devastating effect on our society in general. So, for this very reason as a minimum, government seems to have begun a very complete and thorough program to suppress the evidence of alien visitation.

However, the problem was that there has been evidence of these "others" available to anyone who reads for hundreds of years. Certainly, on the assumption that these creatures exist, it must be asked where do they come from? Clearly, whether these craft and entities come from their home civilization or from bases hidden nearby, the location of said bases is a question of major importance.

With all of that being said, there is one location that stands out as a perfect location from which to observe this planet. That location? Why the Moon of course. Of course, we have been assured that from our space flights and two landings that there is no one on the moon, but can we be sure? Is there evidence to the contrary? Well, surprisingly enough that is a great deal of evidence that NASA is not telling is the truth about what is on the moon as we shall see in the next chapter.

CHAPTER FOUR

SUPPORT FOR THE EXISTENCE OF UFOS AND ALIEN VISITORS

It is no secret that the United States Government is adamant that every UFO reported is a case of mistaken identity or a hoax. In fact, generally, if the sighting can't be dismissed, that the witnesses are attacked publicly as either having a mental problem or seeking publicity. But do all highly placed individuals either in or affiliated with government have the same belief.

The 2016 Presidential election saw the release of thousands of emails of various individuals and organization by a group called Wikileaks run by a man named Julian Assange. His organization hacked the email servers of hundreds and released the information to the public. These emails covered numerous topics that were given major media coverage. However, one area that was discussed in these emails that was virtually ignored by the media were Unidentified Flying Objects (UFOs)[8].

In keeping with what seems to be U.S. Government policy, when the emails released on this topic by Wikileaks could not be refuted, a concert effort was made to target Julian Assange. He was accused of having committed rape in Sweden and this fact was trumpeted from the rooftops by the media in the United States. Of course, it was later determined that he was not charged with rape, but with something called "sex by surprise" or unexpected sex"[9]. Basically, the cause of these charges stemmed from his failure to have used a condemn, a far crime from rape.

According to James Catlin, a lawyer who had represented Assange one of the accusers appeared to have

---

[8] Carlson, Gil, UFO Secrets Spilled by Wikileaks, Blue Planet Press, 2016.
[9] IBID

had tied to US financed anti-Castro and anti-communist groups. In other words, she had tied to the intelligence community who were busting a gut to suppress the release of the Wikileaks emails. Surprise, Surprise!

The true revelation regarding UFOs headlined in these emails is the fact that UFOs have been and are still being seriously discussed in highly classified documents. These emails show beyond a shadow of a doubt that at the very same time our government is assuring us that UFOs are figments of our collective imaginations, they are discussing these figments in these highly classified missives. So now let us look at some of the people whose emails or public statements have contained UFO related material.

WILLIAM JEFFERSON (BILL) CLINTON

In April of 2014, William Jefferson, (Bill) Clinton appeared on the night time talk show, *Jimmy Kimmel Live*. During the interview, Kimmel said *"I probably wouldn't finish the oath. I would run to the White House. I'd demand to see all of the classified files on the UFOs because I want to know. I want to know what has been going on. Did you do that?*"[10]

Clinton replied, "Sort of." He then went on to explain that he had looked into the alleged crash of a UFO in Roswell, New Mexico" in 1947 and into the legends about alien craft being hidden in Area 51. In both cases, he said he found nothing of interest. However, he also made mention of the possibility that there might be career bureaucrats keeping secrets even from the President,

HILLARY RODHAM CLINTON

It is most interesting that two-time Presidential candidate, Hillary Rodham Clinton, former first lady and purported co-President with her husband William Jefferson Clinton wanted very much to discuss UFOs on "***Jimmy Kimmel Live***" during her campaign against President Trump.

---

[10] Openminds.tv

During an interview with reporter Daymond Steer of the ***Conway Daily Sun***,[11] she was asked about her husband's comments regarding UFOs. Her response was very enlightening. She said that *"I think we may have been visited already, but we don't know for sure."*

She also said that her campaign chairman, John Podesta[12], had encouraged her to pursue the subject and noted that he had made her personally pledge *"we are going to get the information out."*

JOHN PODESTA

As noted above, John Podesta is not just some guy in Washington, D.C., but rather a man who has served at the highest levels of our elected government. Not only was he a former councilor to President Barack Obama and White

---

[11] The Conway Daily Sun is a free daily newspaper published in Conway, New Hampshire. Hilly Clinton joined one of their editorial board meetings. When questioned, she promised that, if elected, she would look into UFOS, Area 51 and alien visitation.

[12] John Podesta was not just anyone, but a very highly placed member of the democratic establishment. He was a former councilor to President Barack Obama and White House Chief of Staff for the Clinton Administration.

House Chief of Staff for the Clinton Administration but he was also a major player in the campaign of Hillary Clinton.

Podesta has long discussed his interest in the question of UFOs and aliens. In a press conference in 2002, he publicly called for the release of secret government UFO files. At that time, he said that it is time for government to declassify records that are more than 25 years old and to provide scientists with data that will assist in determining the real nature of this phenomenon[13].

TOM DeLONGE

Tom DeLonge was the guitarist for the power punk trio known as **Blink 182**[14]. It also seems that he had a very serious interest in UFOs. In an email from October 2016, Tom DeLonge wrote to John Podesta that he had been working with a former military official. According to DeLonge, this military official *"wanted to get the word out*

---

[13] Openminds.tv
[14] Blink 182 is an American rock bank formed in Poway, California in 1992.

as he was in charge of all of the stuff. When Roswell crashed, they shipped it to the laboratory at Wright Patterson Air Force Base. General McCasland[15] was in charge of that exact laboratory up to a couple of years ago."

Further emails also reveal that Tom DeLong is also being advised by 10 high level insiders who want to reveal the truth behind a secret space program being run out of Area 51. Of the ten, we know that one is Major General William McCasland, while another is said to be Rob Weiss, head of Lockheed Martin's Skunk Works while a third is another United States Air Force Major General, Michael Carey.

EDGAR MITCHELL

Edgar Dean (Ed) Mitchell[16] was a United States Naval officer, an aviator, test pilot, aeronautical engineer,

---

[15] Major General William N. McCasland was the commander of the Air Force Research Laboratory and ran the top-secret United States Air Force Research Facility at Wright Patterson Air Force Base until 2013.

[16] Edgar Mitchell was born September 1930 in Hereford, Texas. He held a Bachelor of Science Degree in aeronautical engineering from the U.S. Naval Postgraduate School and a Doctor of Science degree in Aeronautics and Aeronautics from the Massachusetts Institute of Technology. Edgar Mitchell died February 4, 2016.

NASA Astronaut and a firm believer in UFOs. He was also a member of the crew of Apollo 14, the pilot of the Apollo 14 Lunar Lander and the sixth man to walk on the moon. Dr. Mitchell was a firm believer in the existence of UFOS, aliens and the Roswell crash.

In 2014, Dr. Mitchell's representative Terri Mansfield sent an email asking John Podesta for a meeting to discuss how zero-point energy from aliens could save the planet form global warming. The email went on to say that *"we work with specific Extraterrestrial Intelligence (ETI) from a contiguous universe."*

Prior to his death, Dr. Mitchell gave many interviews where he confirmed his belief in the reality of UFOs and aliens.

NATIONAL SECURITY AGENCY (NSA)

There was a discussion in **NSA Technical Journal, Volume XI, No. 1-** by Mr. Lambros D. Callimahos regarding certain aspects of extraterrestrial intelligence. Dr.

Howard H. Campaigne[17] wrote an article for the NSA Technical Journal[18] discussing a series of radio message that had been heard coming from outer space.

Some believe that one of the NSA's original missions was to try and eavesdrop on alien communication. Remember that the NSA was created shortly after the crash at Roswell. Coincidence?

NATIONAL AERONAUTICS AND SPACE ADMINISTRATION (NASA)

NASA has long held out the belief that the Moon is just a cold, airless, lifeless rock and is not inhabited and has never been inhabited. Of course, if this is really the case, then why has NASA shown such interest in what takes place on the moon. Remember, we actually dropped a nuclear device on the moon, allegedly looking for water.

---

[17] Dr. Campaigne is a mathematician and cryptographer who served during World War II at OP-20-G and for a short time at Benchley Park.
[18] This article was released as a result of a FOIA request, cited as Case #41472. It was approved for release by the NSA on October 21, 2004.

Then of course there are the secret back channels used by the Astronauts to report things that they do not want the public to know. There have been many reports heard of Astronauts sighting strange things in space that have been cut off in mid-word as the conversations switched to these secret back channels. It was allegedly Astronaut Scott Carpenter who said that at no time, when the astronauts were in space were they alone: there was a constant surveillance by UFOs.

However, let us look at some communications said to come from NASA. During the 1969 moon landings, the entire event was televised for the entire world to see and all radio communications between the astronauts on the Moon and the earth were clearly heard by the avid listeners on the earth, or rather that is what NASA wanted us to think.

If the reader will recall, the first two men to walk on the Moon were Neil Armstrong and Buzz Aldrin. The following conversation between Armstrong, Aldrin and

Mission Control was released by Christopher Kraft[19], director of the NASA Mission Control in Houston during the Apollo Moon missions after his retirement[20].

ASTRONAUTS: *"These are giant things. No, No, No – this is not an optical illusion.*

MISSION CONTROL: *"What... What...what? What the hell is happening? What's wrong with you?*

ASTRONAUTS: *"They are here, under the surface."*

MISSION CONTROL: *"What's there? Emission interrupted... interference control calling Apollo 11."*

ASTRONAUTS: *"We saw some visitors. They were there for a while, observing the instruments."*

MISSION CONTROL: *"Repeat your last information."*

ASTRONAUTS: *"I say that there were other spaceships. They're lined up on the other side of the crater."*

MISSION CONTROL: *"Repeat...Repeat!"*

---

[19] Christopher Columbus (Chris) Kraft, Jr. became NASA's first flight director. He was on duty during the Apollo 11 Mission to the Moon.
[20] Carlson, Gil, Aliens on the Moon, Blue Planet Press, 2017

ASTRONAUTS: "*Let us sound this orbita. . . .In 625 to 5. . .automatic relay connected. . . My hands are shaking so badly I can't do anything. Film it? God, if those damned cameras have picked up anything. . .what then?*"

MISSION CONTROL: "*Have you picked up anything?*"

ASTRONAUTS: "*I don't have any film at hand. Three shots of the saucers or whatever they were that were ruining the film.*"

MISSION CONTROL: "*Control, Control here. Are you on your way? Is the uproar with the UFOs over?*"

ASTRONAUTS: "*They have landed there. There they are, and they are watching us.*"

MISSION CONTROL: "*The mirrors, the mirrors . . .have you set them up?*"

ASTRONAUTS: "*Yes, they're in the right place. But whoever made those space ships surely can come tomorrow and remove them. Over and out.*"

NASA makes no secret of the fact that the missions, both manned as well as unmanned, have taken literally tens of thousands of photos. Though paid for by tax payer dollars, they are archived and not discussed. However, what is not openly discussed is that there is an entire building dedicated to airbrushing these photos before they are released to the public, if they are ever released to the public.

What is there about the moon that our leaders do not want us to know? Let's look at some facts about the Moon in the next chapter.

CHAPTER FIVE
FACTS ABOUT THE MOON

There are many mysteries about the moon. First, scientists don't know how the Moon was created. There are actually two school of thought as to how the Moon was formed. The first school of thought is the "Big Whack" theory. That is something hit the earth millions of years ago creating a cloud of debris that eventually came together to create the Moon.

The second school of thought is that the Moon broke off from the earth while the planet was still in a molten stage. This broken off mass was believed to be spinning so fast it formed into a dumbbell shape and one end broke off[21]. However, notice that both of these theories presuppose that at one time the Earth and the Moon were part of the same body.

It should be remembered that one of the accomplishments of Apollo 11 was the collection of a number of moon rocks. A thorough study of the harvested rocks revealed that some of the Moon rocks were over a billion years older than the Earth and that the moon dust that coats its surface was a billion years older than the rocks.

A new study found that the Moon is believed to be 4.51 to 4.6 billion years old[22]. The Earth is thought to be approximately 4.543 billion years old. With that being said there was a report in **Sky and Telescope**[23] that one moon

---

[21] This theory was formed by Sir George Darwin in 1880. He was the son of Charles Darwin, the creator of Darwin's Theory of Evolution, which never been conclusively proven to this day.
[22] Space.com
[23] SKYANDTELESCOPE.COM – this finding came from a lunar conference in 1973.

rock was found to be approximately 5.3 Billion years old, approximately a billion yards older than our planet.

Consider also that the Moon's orbit is almost a perfect circle and that one side is always turned away from the earth. Interestingly enough, these two characteristics are not found in regard to any other natural body in space but are usually associated with artificial satellites.

Another interesting finding was that chemical analysis showed that the composition of the Moon rocks and the moon dust were completely different from each other. In fact, they were not even closely related to each other as would certainly have expected. What all of this means is that the Moon may have been created somewhere else in the cosmos and was not a part of the earth as previously believed. It also means that some of the Moon rocks were placed on the surface of the moon long after the dust that covers the surface was created.

Additionally, anomalies were also discovered. Some of the rock samples recovered by the Soviets in 1970 were even found to be completely resistant to rust. This technology was not known to man at the time and was years ahead of Earth technology.

THE MOON IS NOT FROM HERE

Based on all of this rather recent research, it is now well accepted that the Moon originated elsewhere in the universe and was somehow moved into the earth's orbit. Isaac Asimov stated that the Moon was too large to have been captured by the earth's gravitational field and moved into such a perfect orbit.

Zecharia Sitchin wrote in his book *"Genesis Revisited*[24]*"* that some of the answers regarding the moon are provided if we research the Sumerian cosmology. According to the Sumerians, one of the eleven Moons of Tiamat[25],

---

[24] Sitchin, Zecharia, Genesis Revisited, Simon & Schuster, New York, 1990.
[25] Tiamat was the name of the planet that previously occupied Earth's orbit.

named Kingu, grew to an unusual size and became increasing disruptive to the other Planets of the solar system. In the ensuing period of instability, the planet Tiamat was split into two pieces. One half was completely shattered and became the asteroid belt and the other half, accompanied by Kingu, stabilized a new orbit to become Earth and its Moon.

Assuming that Sitchin is correct about the Sumerian cosmology regarding the Moon it now becomes clear that none of our scientific theories about the Moon are correct. So, its origin is still in doubt, but that is not the only mystery that revolves around our Moon. How about its composition.

Scientists have long called the Moon a dead rock in space. However, when the Apollo astronauts drilled into the surface of the moon in order to inserts probes to monitor the moon's temperature, they brought up metal shavings not pieces of rock[26]. This data comes from so-called heat-flow

---

[26] Business Insider, "A 40-year old mystery about rising temperatures on the moon has been solved – and it was probably the Apollo astronauts' fault." BusinessInsider.com

experiments that were conducted on the moon in 1971 and 1972 by members of the Apollo 15 and Apollo 17 Missions.

For these experiments, the astronauts drilled two holes into the surface at depths ranging anywhere between 3.2 feet and 7.5 feet deep. Fiberglass tubes were inserted into the holes and platinum thermometers were placed inside the tubes to read the temperatures at varying depths below the surface.

It was noticed in 1975 that the thermometers recorded an unusual warming on the surface of the moon some four years after the probes were inserted. Researchers believe that the men who walked on the moon may have caused this increase in temperature. There were a number of other theories, but each is more bizarre than the one before. Of course, if some of the theories that this writer will discuss are true, there is a simple answer for this increase in temperature as we shall see.

It is also interesting to note that there are hundreds of moonquakes each year that cannot be ascribed to any particular cause, which leads us to the question, what is the interior of moon like.

On November 19, 1969, the Apollo 12 lunar lander, Intrepid landed on the moon. Astronauts Alan Bean and Pete Conrad landed on the moon to conduct a new round of experiments and some very interesting things were discovered.

From the website history.nasa.gov comes a history of the **Apollo Expeditions to the Moon**[27]. Chapter 12.3 is especially interesting in that it confirms a number of the so-called tall tales about the moon. The two Apollo 12 Astronauts examined the crash site of Surveyor 3 which crashed in 1967.

According to the two Apollo 12 astronauts, Surveyor was covered with a coating of fine dust that looked to be tan

---

[27] History.nsa.gov

or perhaps brown in the lunar light. The craft was no long the pristine white it had been when it left earth orbit. Scientists, not wanting to "speculate," speculated that Surveyor became covered in this fashion when the dust on the Moon was kicked up by the landing of Apollo 12 even though the landing site was over 600 feet away.

The Apollo 12 astronauts took samples from the Surveyor 3 wreckage for study on earth. They cut samples of the aluminum tubing which seemed much more brittle than it had on earth. They also cut samples of electrical cables which later examination showed had gotten dry, hard and brittle.

THE MOON RANG LIKE A GONG

Once the Moon walkers returned to their command module, after some experiments it was decided to jettison the landing module which was planned to be crashed into the moon[28]. According to the testing equipment, the Moon rang like a gong, vibrating and resonating for almost an hour after the crash. From this is was deduced that the core of the Moon may not be solid, but rather somewhat hollow.

When Apollo 14 jettisoned their lunar module, Antares, this same phenomenon was observed at two ALSEP stations. In fact, on every mission after Apollo 12, additional seismic calibrations were obtained by aiming the Saturn S-IVB stage to impact at a selected point on the moon. The vibrations generally lasted about three hours.

Based on these experiments, it can only be concluded that the core of the Moon is not solid, giving rise to speculation that the interior of the moon may be hollow.

THE MOON'S COMPOSITION

Research has determined that the Moon has three distinct layers of rock. Now we have always been taught that

---

[28] One reason for crashing the landing module was that they had placed a number of seismic recording devices on the surface and they wanted to see what they would record regarding this crash.

in the formation of our planet, the heavier rocks sink toward the core and the lighter rocks are found on the surface. However, according to the author of "**Our Mysterious Spaceship Moon,**" Don Wilson, all of these anomalies had been carefully studied by two Soviet scientists, Michael Vasin and Alexander Shcherbakov[29]. Their research caused them to propose what came to be called the **Artificial Moon Theory** that the Moon was a hollowed-out spaceship.

Further support for this somewhat outlandish theory came from an article published in the July 1962 issue of **Astronautics Magazine**. In this article, Dr. Gordon MacDonald[30], who was a leading scientist at NASA at the time, stated that according to an analysis of the Moon's motion, it spears that the Moon is hollow. He went on to say that if the astronomical date is reduced it is found that the date requires that the interior of the Moon be less dense than

---

[29] Members of the Soviet Academy of Sciences.
[30] Gordon James Fraser MacDonald, (1929 – 2002)

the outer parts. Indeed, he said, it would seem that the Moon is more like a hollow sphere than a homogenous sphere.

If as the Soviet scientist propose the Moon is a hollowed-out spaceship, then the hull would have to be tremendously strong. But arguing against that is the very observable fact that meteors have bombarded the surface of the Moon since time immemorable.

While this would seem to be a problem to the theory that the Moon is a hollow sphere, it is interesting to note that even the largest craters caused by what are apparently meteor crashes are unusually shallow. Craters that are fifty to a hundred miles across are generally no more than 2 or 3 miles deep.

Research has shown that a meteor weighing a million tons would hit the surface of the moon with an explosive force equal to a one megaton atomic bomb. However, there is little doubt that meteors weighing a million tons has hit the lunar surface time and time again but left only broad shallow craters.

However, scientific research has shown that meteors 10 miles or more in diameter should have penetrated the surface to a depth of 4 or 5 times that diameter, however, the deepest Moon crater found to date[31] is 186 miles across and yet less than 4 miles deep.

After looking at all of the evidence, scientists could only conclude that beneath the Moon's surface is something extremely strong and tough that can resist penetration by such high impact explosives. Some have suggested that this may be the interior hull of a hidden space craft.

AND SO

So, the evidence seems to support the fact that the Moon may be hollow with an incredibly tough inner hull of some type. Well there have been theories that the Earth is hollow and, so far, that has not been proven to be true. So,

---

[31] The Gagarin Crater

let us look to see if there might be any evidence that there are inhabitants on or closest neighbor in space.

CHAPTER SIX
STRANGE ACTIVITY ON THE MOON

In spite of all of the assurance we have received from our scientific leaders that the Moon is basically dead. A rock orbiting the Earth, there is a large body of evidence that there is something going on both on the surface of and inside this "dead" rock. Let us look at some of these very unusual anomalies that were recorded and reported by Don Wilson in his interesting book "*Our Mysterious Spaceship Moon.*[32]".

- In the year 1843, astronomer Johann Schroeter recorded a crater six-miles wide on the surface of the moon that he called **Linne**. Its depth was estimated

---

[32] Wilson, Don, Our Mysterious Spaceship Moon, Sphere Books Ltd. 1976.

to be some 1200 feet. Today Linne is a tiny bright spot with very little depth, just a small pit surrounded by a number of whitish objects. To date no one come up with an explanation for how the crater was filled in or has identified the whitish objects.

- As our closest neighbor, the Moon has been studied by every type of scientist on the planet, certainly by astronomers from every country. Many of these scientists also listen intently for any sign that there are signals coming from space. It is not too surprising that many of these scientists hear strange messages from space.

- In 1935, two scientists by the name of Van der Pol[33] and Carl Stormer[34] heard radio signals both coming from the surface as well the area around the Moon. Marconi[35] and Tesla[36] also reported flashing lunar

---

[33] A physicist and the developer of the famous equation of Van Der Pol.
[34] An Astrophysicist
[35] Guglielmo Marconi
[36] Nikola Tesla

lights originating from this supposedly dead rock in space.

- In 1956, scientists at Ohio University, as well as numerous observatories around the globe, reported hearing a codelike chatter coming from the Moon.

- In 1958, astronomers from America, Russia and Great Britain spotted something speeding toward the Moon at over 25,000 miles per hour. These astronomers also detected radio signals that no one could decipher coming from this mysterious craft.

Naturally, Don Wilson was not the only one to comment on strange things seen on or around the Moon. In the 1950s numerous Unidentified Flying Objects (UFOs) were tracked to the Moon by government tracking stations. In the 1950s and 1960s moving as well as flashing lights were seen on the lunar surface by civilian astronomers. Usually these lights were seen inside craters.

Though there is a great deal of photographic evidence of activity on the Moon, NASA has gone to great lengths to cover up as much as they can. Unfortunately, for NASA, both Soviet as well as American spacecraft in orbit around the Moon began to photograph mysterious structures on the Moon.

It was American spacecraft Ranger II that took over 200 photographs of the Moon that showed domes erected inside some of the craters. French Astronomers reported in the news media seeing these mysterious domes over 50 years ago. You must ask yourself, who is building domes on the Moon? Lunar Orbiter 2 took 33 photos of domes on the Moon that were released in Washington DC in 1967.

HAVE WE FOUND CITIES ON THE MOON?

As strange as it may seem, NASA has admitted that we found man-made structures on the moon. This took place during a briefing at the Washington National Press Club on March 21, 1996. At that time, NASA scientists and engineers who took part in the exploration of Mars and the Moon reported that for the first time, manmade structures and other objects have been discovered on the moon.

There are also numerous former NASA employees who have revealed that all NASA photos are carefully examined and any UFOs or anything that would tend to confirm the belief that there are entities living on the moon that may have been caught in the picture are airbrushed out before the photo is added to the catalog. Clearly, there is some fear at NASA that we may find proof that UFOs exist. In fact, unusual artifacts that should not exist if the Moon is a dead rock have been discovered in 44 different regions.

According to Richard Hoagland, the ruins of lunar cities that stretch for many kilometers have been photographed as well as huge domes at or near some of the major craters that dot the surface of the Moon. There is even one NASA photograph of Copernicus Crater[37] that shows a

---

[37] Image PIA00094

bright self-illuminating object in the distance that resembles a tower. There was also a transparent dome photographed on the edge of Copernicus Crater that glows white and blue from the inside.

As if that was not enough, this author was once asked by a listener[38] to order a specific picture from NASA. The picture showed a track vehicle rolling across the surface of the Moon. However, the date of the photo was at a tie that no one was supposed to be on the Moon. I asked NASA to explain the photo, however, rather than answer, they said that they would get back to me, but they never did.

Unfortunately, our government has taken the position that we are not ready to know the truth about what flies in our skies, though there has been some leaking of information. However, in spite of our own government's

---

[38] Adventure Radio, KORG Radio, Anaheim, CA. (Today my show is The Ken Hudnall Show, on the Internet at Kenhudnall.com)

refusal to admit the reality of UFOs, there has been evidence that has been hard for them to coverup.

For example, on July 19, 1952, a veritable fleet of UFOs flew over the White House, the Capital Building and the Department of Defense. It happened a second time on July 25, 1952. In spite of the numerous photos and stories in the major main stream media, the government down played the event.

CHAPTER SEVEN
BEHIND THE SCENES

We are told by our government that we do not even formally research UFO sightings any loner as there are no such things as flying saucers. However, there are numerous stories that in the face of this blatant activity by the power behind the UFOs that our leaders actually met with representatives of this alien power to discuss a treaty. While many continue to discount the very idea of such a meeting, there are persistent stories that cannot be discounted out of hand.

It has long been reported that in fear that there might be an alien attack, that President Harry S. Truman ordered the military to contact these entities to arrange the release of an alien captured by the U.S. Military at one of the crash sites. Then later in 1952, it was reported that Truman ordered the C.I.A.[39] and later the NSA[40] to broadcast a message to the aliens that we wanted to meet with them to discuss a treaty. The C.I.A. and the Cipher Bureau, which became the NSA, worked to carry out the President's directive of trying to contact the alien. This program became known as Project SIGMA which began in 1952.

PROJECT SIGMA

Though authorized in 1952 by President Truman, it was not until 1953 under President Eisenhower that Project SIGMA was successful. According to William Milton (Bill) Cooper, it was under Project SIGMA that humans first established communications with the aliens and he claimed that the project was still in existence. Allegedly using

---

[39] It should be remembered that President Truman signed the National Security Act of 1947 in September of 1947, only 76 days after the crash of an alien craft at Roswell, New Mexico. There are those that do not believe it was a coincidence.

[40] What became known as the National Security Agency had its beginnings on April 28, 1917 as the Cipher Bureau, created shortly after the begining of World War I, it became the NSA in 1952.

communications equipment salvaged from crashed UFOs, messages were beamed to several huge ships that radar revealed were in orbit around our planet.

Bill Cooper went on to report that from Project SIGMA came Project PLATO, which was given the responsibility for establishing diplomatic relations with the alien beings. Project PLATO was said to be created in 1953 at the time contact was first made with the alien beings

Under the auspices of Project PLATO. On February 20, 1954, Project PLATO agreed to a formal treaty[41] with the aliens which was signed by President Eisenhower. Under the terms of this treaty, the U.S. Government would receive technology and in return it would keep the alien presence a secret and not interfere in any way with anything the aliens decided to do. The aliens were also allowed to abduct

---

[41] Under the U.S. Constitution, this treaty was illegal as it was never formally ratified by Congress.

humans and animals though the aliens did agree to furnish the government with a list of those abducted[42].

PROJECT CRYSTAL KNIGHT

According to Bill Cooper, Project CRYSTAL KNIGHT was the name given to the exchange of ambassadors between humans and Extraterrestrial Biological Entities (EBENs). It was reported that twelve people were selected in 1965 and sent for 13 years to what was reported to be the planet of the EBEs. This exchange was said to have run from 1954 to 1978. It was reported that only eight of the twelve returned to the earth. Two died, two wanted to stay and the remaining eight came back to earth.

HOLLOMAN AIR FORCE BASE

It has also been reported by researcher Val Valerian that the treaty was renewed on April 25, 1964 during a meeting at Holloman Air Force Base, New Mexico. So, assuming these stories do have the ring of truth, it would

---

[42] Exopaedia.org

seem that these aliens have been among us, formally, for over 60 years with legal (or otherwise) sanction by our government.

The very idea that we have a treaty with aliens brings rise to a number of questions. For example, could some of them be living among us? This concept is not ore unbelievable that that they exist in the first place.

Consider, if you will, that we have all met people we consider strange. Especially in the big city there have been stories about truly unbelievable people who livened very strange lives. Could they be aliens, or perhaps hybrids[43]? Certainly, the very idea of contact between man and some sort of mimicking entity are not rare. In fact, such contacts number in the millions throughout history. I might also point out, at the risk of causing coronary arrest among those who are rabid believers in our world's religions that the very

---

[43] Keel, John, Our Haunted Planet, Fawcett Gold Metal Books, Greenwich, Comm. 1971.,

concept of most religions are based on the very concept that man has been a higher being, call it God, or an angel or Hairy the Hairy Ape, the concept still remains a human met something extremely weird, by earthly standards, and interacted with it[44].

Even early man was well aware of the possibility that he (or she) could come in contact with those who were not exactly human. In **Hebrews Chapter 13, verse 2**[45] the Bible warns to *"Be not forgetful to entertain strangers, for thereby some have entertained angels unaware."*

So, we must ask at this point, what is an angel? Most angels in the Bible are described as looking like ordinary man. The idea that angels have wings was an artistic concept to make it clear that they were something beyond the ordinary. I would submit that at its basic definition that an

---

[44] Ibid
[45] Holy Bible, King James Edition.

angel is a representative of a higher power. Be that higher power a God or a more powerful entity than a mere human.

It should be noted that there are literally thousands of stories of interaction between human kind and, for lack of a better term, inhuman kind. Now setting aside the strangeness for a moment, we must ask some very practical questions. Where do all of these odd creatures live that are wandering our planet?

While there are places in this world that are rarely visited by educated man, in the US there are few places that are not at least regularly passed through. But a place that would certainly fit the bill as a home for these mysterious entities would be the Moon.

CHAPTER EIGHT

WHAT CAUSED SUSPICION THERE MIGHT BE LIFE ON THE MOON?

Science has long taught us that there cannot be any life on the Moon as it is an airless rock floating in space. So why might we think that there might be life on the moon?

The concept that there might be some type of life on the Moon began when Marconi, the inventor of the radio reported that his experiments in transmitting radio signals to the Moon resulted in his receiving answering signals. Shortly after that, in the 1920s and 1930s, astronomers in America, Britain and France reported seeing glowing, moving and even blinking lights on the surface of the Moon.

Then interest peaked when, in the early 1950s, John O'Neill, an expert in aerial phenomenon and a Pulitzer Prize winning astronomer reported seeing a lighted bridge on the Moon that he believed was built by a mysterious intelligence. Numerous other astronomers began to survey the same area of the moon where O'Neill had seen the twelve-mile-long bridge and were forced to admit that he had in fact seen such an oddity on the surface of our deserted moon[46].

It should also be noted that during the 1950s and even into the 1960s, there were many UFOs that were tracked by both civilian astronomers as well as government tracking stations traveling from the earth to the Moon[47]. Certainly, a moon base would be the perfect place to hide a fleet of UFOs.

From the latter part of the 1950s into the 1960s, a number of astronomers have recorded moving, flashing and stationary lights on the surface of the Moon. It should be

---

[46] The bridge was later dismantled by the same intelligence that built it.
[47] Appendix A is a NASA Technical Report that lists activity on the Moon from the mid 1500s to 1968. It seems our deserted Moon has been pretty busy over the years.

noted that much of this activity seemed to be concentrated inside the craters doting the surface of our satellite.

BUZZ ALDRIN'S ADVENTURES

So, it was, that with a massive expenditure of time and resources, the United States landed a man on the Moon in 1969. Much like Columbus landing in the New World, it was time to plant our flag as a sign of conquest and break out the champagne. Or maybe not! There is evidence that we were not the first on the Moon.

There is a report that when Buzz Aldrin opened the door of the Lunar Lander, he found himself staring at a sentient creature that seemed as surprised to see him as he was to see it[48]. It should be noted that there were a number of communications that were hard to understand between the astronauts on the moon and Houston. Perhaps this can be explained by something said by NASA Director, Kraft when he commented on the fact that there was both a public as well

---

[48] Carlson, Gil, Aliens on the Moon, Blue Planet Press, 2017

as a private radio channel between the Moon and Mission Control.

This private radio channel was certainly in support of the requirement that if NASA discovered anything that would tend to support the existence of other life forms it was to remain classified[49].

It was noted that at the moment of landing, there was a mysterious two-minute interruption between the men on the moon and Mission Control. Perhaps this creature was the topic of conversation.

I have also heard mention of this strange communication from a number of Ham radio operators who had VHF equipment allowing them to listen directly to the Astronaut communications and heard the discussion of the creature Aldrin is alleged to have seen. Even Ham radio operators in Russia are reported to have heard these censored

---

[49] Few seem to realize that the "civilian space agency" was actually an arm of the Department of Defense.

communications and quickly published the information in Moscow that there were creatures on the moon.

OBSERVATIONS BY OTHER ASTRONAUTS

In spite of the efforts by NASA Mission Control to censor the communications from Apollo 11, apparently there was a slip up in regard to communications from Apollo 15 when Astronaut James Irwin, the lunar module pilot, talked about *"domes structures are partially filled up, Breach has either flowed into these structures before they were built, or the domes are younger than the floor. The area is oval or elliptical."*

Other communications talked about "**flashes of light**", "**buildings**", "**roads**", "**tracks**" and "**huge blocks**". At one point, he also made the comment that "**that's the most organized structure I've ever seen.**"

Of course, when space program officials were asked about the comments, they were told that the comments by

James Irwin were metaphors for geological formations[50]. Clearly, someone thinks that the man on the street is an imbecile.

AL WORDEN

While James Irwin was touring domes on the surface of the Moon, Al Worden, the Command Module Pilot for Apollo 15, was having his own interactions with someone or something on the Moon. According to Worden at 11:15 there was an unusual fading of communications with Mission Control. Worden reported that he then heard a breathing sound and a long whistle. Then there was a sentence constantly repeated on one note, varying from a small to a shrill tone and from lightly stressed sounds to raucous exclamations. The Lem's tape recorder captured the message and, when communications were re-established, Worden transmitted it to NASA[51].

---

[50] Ibid
[51] It is interesting to note that his transmissions to Mission Control was also heard on French public television though this should have been impossible.

The message recorded and transmitted to Mission control consisted of eight words in an unknown language. The message was "**MARA RABBI ALLARDI DINI ENDAVOUR ESA COUNS ALIM.**" It has never been transmitted, or if it has, the meaning has never been released by NASA.

NEIL ARMSTRONG

There is a comment that has long been attributed to Neil Armstrong. He is purported to have said that *"We were ordered to Move Away by Aliens on the Moon."*

According to reports, speaking unofficially, Armstrong said, "We were warned away." "I cannot go into details, except to say that their ships were far superior to ours both in size and technology. They were great and threatening."

WATER ON THE MOON

On the 25th day of January 1994, the Clementine Mission was launched as a joint project between the

Strategic Defense Initiative Organization (SDI) and NASA. The stated mission was to explore other areas of the Moon and take photographs.

When scientists reviewed the data from Clementine, they discovered that, contrary to our basic beliefs about the Moon, ice existed inside some of the moon's craters. This finding was further confirmed in early 1998 by NASA's Lunar Prospector. Now I am not a scientist, but I do know that if there is ice, then there is liquid, probably water, on the moon[52], something we were assured could not be true.

In addition to this came a statement form Dr. John Brandenburg, Deputy Manager of the Clementine Mission[53]. In an interview, Dr. Brandenburg[54] stated that *"the Clementine Mission was a photo reconnaissance mission basically to check out if someone was building bases on the*

---

[52] There have been a number of sightings of water vapor coming from the surface of the Moon,
[53] Exxonews.org
[54] Spudislunarresources.com

moon that we didn't know about. Were they expanding them?"

Dr. Brandenburg went on to say: *"Of all the pictures I've seen from the moon that show possible structures, the most impressive is a picture of miles wide recto-linear structure. This looks unmistakably artificial and it shouldn't be there. As somebody in the space defense community, I look on any such structure on the moon with great concern because it isn't ours, there's no way we could have built such a thing. It means that someone else is up there!"*

DID NASA BOMB THE MOON

It is also interesting to note that, though it has been kept very quiet, NASA released a 2-ton "Centaur" kinetic weapon that impacted on the Moon on October 9, 2009[55]. It was said that this was done for scientific purposes, but there is are a large number of people who believe that this was

---

[55] For those not familiar with this type of weapon, a kinetic bombardment is the act of attacking a planetary surface with an inert projectile, where the destructive force comes from the kinetic energy of the projectile impacting at very high velocities.

done to destroy a number of alien structures that had been built on the surface of the Moon.

It should also be noted that some of the very ancient craters on the Moon's surface resemble nuclear bomb craters more than they do craters left by asteroids. Perhaps we are not the first ones to bomb the surface of the Moon.

It is also claimed by a former NASA employee, Clark McClelland that mining operations were observed by the Apollo 15 Astronaut Crew. Of Course, nothing was said to the general public. If someone is mining the moon, then clearly, they have established some control over our satellite and feel secure in conducting their operations. Of course, the primary questions are:

1. What is being mined? and
2. Who is mining it?

CHAPTER NINE
A FINAL POSSIBILITY

Certainly, the activity that has been spotted on the Moon since the mid 1500s could be, and probably are, other life forms, the very existence of which is kept as a very closely held secret. However, there is one other possibility that needs to be seriously discussed. It is common knowledge that any technology demonstrated by our government is one, possible two years obsolete. Therefore, it is certainly possible that our space program is also obsolete, which leads to some very interesting questions.

Earlier in this volume we have talked at length about the possibility that the U.S. Government has demonstrated a great deal of concern about these lights in the sky. In fact, in

1952, after a fleet of UFOs buzzed he capitol, President Truman is alleged to have given the CIA the order to contact the entities flying these mysterious craft. Then there were further reports that President Eisenhower even entered into a treaty with these entities.

So, it these UFOs were and are looked at as a threat, then logically, our military would begin to look at a way to prepare for interaction with these entities. Therefore, we need to look at what, if anything, our military did that might relate to readiness for deal with UFOs.

It will certainly surprise many that in March of 1959, Project Horizon was undertaken to develop and build a permanent lunar outpost. According to a letter signed by Lieutenant General Arthur G. Trudeau[56], Chief of Research and Development for the General Staff, on March 30, 1959 and sent to the Chief of Ordinance of the Department of the

---

[56] In 1958, LTG Trudeau served as Director of Army Research and Development.

Army, there was a requirement for a manned military outpost on the moon. This outpost was required to develop and protect potential United States interests on the moon; development techniques in moon-based surveillance of the earth and space, in communications relay, and in operations on the surface of the moon; to serve as a base for exploration of the moon, for further exploration into space and for military operations on the moon if required; and to support scientific investigations on the moon.

It is also interesting that in his letter, LTG Trudeau made it clear that there are no known technical barriers to establishing a manned outpost on the Moon. If this is true, then perhaps there is currently a manned outpost monitoring both the earth as well as outer space. It is most certainly true that the description of the structure discussed in Project Horizon materials and carefully outlined in the military's proposal for the building of the manned lunar outpost seems to mirror, in many respects, some of the structures caught in some of NASA's lunar photos.

Certainly, the story put forward by Alternative 3[57] would seem to indicate that both the, then, Soviet Union as well as the US had manned installations established on the Moon as well as in alleged colonies said to be located on the planet Mars.

We will discuss Alternative 3 and its ties to some of the worldwide disappearances of those with a technical background in a future volume. For now, we must be satisfied with the assertion that the plot outlined in this unusual book supports, in many respects, the idea that there is life on the Moon.

Frankly, the establish the validity that there is life on the Moon it would only take one unexplainable sighting of activity on the surface of the Moon. However, at Appendix

---

[57] Watkins, Leslie, Alternative 3, 1978.

A are literally hundreds of sightings that covered over 400 years. Enjoy.

Clearly, it does not take much in the way of investigative ability to be able to look at lights and movements in an area that it not supposed to have lights or movements and be able to determine that there is someone, or something, present. So, it is that, in spite of all of NASA's denials, there is verifiable proof that there is someone on the Moon. The question is, are these Moon people human or alien?

APPENDIX A

CHRONOLOGICAL CATALOG OF REPORTED LUNAR EVENTS[58]

The attached technical report[59] from NASA is a catalog of sightings of unusual activity on the Moon at a time when no one is supposed to have been on the Moon. This report is solid proof that someone has been on the Moon since at least the year 1540 through 1968. It makes one wonder how much earlier in our history there was identified activity on the Moon that we did not know to look for or even have the ability to see.

---

[58] NASA Technical Report R-277
[59] It should be kept in mind that a government agency cannot copyright a publication as it is paid for with taxpayer dollars, thus it is in the public domain.

A TECHNICAL REPORT  NASA TR R-277

NASA TR R-277

CHRONOLOGICAL CATALOG
OF REPORTED LUNAR EVENTS

by

Barbara M. Middlehurst
University of Arizona

Jaylee M. Burley
Goddard Space Flight Center

Patrick Moore
Armagh Planetarium

and

Barbara L. Welther
Smithsonian Astrophysical Observatory

NATIONAL AERONAUTICS AND SPACE ADMINISTRATION • WASHINGTON, D. C. • JULY 1968

TECHNICAL REPORT

NASA TR R-277

CHRONOLOGICAL CATALOG OF REPORTED LUNAR EVENTS

by

Barbara M. Middlehurst University of Arizona

Jaylee M. Burley
Goddard Space Flight Center

Patrick Moore Armagh Planetarium

and

Barbara L. Welther
Smithsonian Astrophysical Observatory

NATIONAL AERONAUTICS AND SPACE ADMINISTRATION

WASHINGTON, D. C.

JULY 1968

NASA TR R-277

CHRONOLOGICAL CATALOG OF REPORTED LUNAR EVENTS

By

Barbara M. Middlehurst
University of Arizona
Tucson, Ariz.

Jaylee M. Burley
Goddard Space Flight Center
Greenbelt, Md.

Patrick Moore
Armagh Planetarium
Armagh, Northern Ireland

and

Barbara L. Welther
Smithsonian Astrophysical Observatory
Cambridge, Mass.

NATIONAL AERONAUTICS AND SPACE ADMINISTRATION

For sale by the Clearinghouse for Federal Scientific and Technical Information
Springfield, Virginia 22151 – CFSTI price $3.00

CHRONOLOGICAL CATALOG OF REPORTED LUNAR EVENTS

By

Barbara M. Middlehurst University of Arizona Tucson, Ariz.

Jaylee M. Burley Goddard Space Flight Center Greenbelt, Md.

Patrick Moore Armagh Planetarium Armagh, Northern Ireland

and

Barbara L. Welther Smithsonian Astrophysical Observatory Cambridge, Mass.

NATIONAL AERONAUTICS AND SPACE ADMINISTRATION

For sole by the Clearinghouse for Federal Scientific and Technical Information Springfield, Virginia 22151 - CFSTI price $3.00

NASA TR R-277

ABSTRACT

A catalog of reports of lunar events, or temporary changes on the moon, has been compiled based on literature covering more than four centuries. In most cases, the original reference has been consulted; Houzeau and Lancaster's *Bibliographie Général d'Astronomie* and the *Astronomischer Jahresbericht* were useful secondary sources. Each entry includes a brief description and date of the observation, the name of the observer(s), where these are known, and the reference.

ii

ABSTRACT

A catalog of reports of lunar events, or temporary changes on the moon, has been compiled based on literature covering more than four centuries. In most cases, the original reference has been consulted; Houzeau and Lancaster's Bibliographie

General d'Astronomie and the Astronomischer Jahresbericht were useful secondary sources. Each entry includes a brief description and date of the observation, the name of the observers), where these are known, and the reference.

CONTENTS

INTRODUCTION	1
DESCRIPTION OF CATALOG	1
REPORTS OMITTED FROM THE CATALOG	2
ACKNOWLEDGMENTS	3
CHRONOLOGICAL CATALOG OF REPORTED LUNAR EVENTS	5
REFERENCES	45

INTRODUCTION 1 DESCRIPTION OF CATALOG 1
REPORTS OMITTED FROM THE CATALOG 2
ACKNOWLEDGMENTS 3 CHRONOLOGICAL CATALOG OF REPORTED

LUNAR EVENTS REFERENCES

Frontispiece: Topographical distribution of reported lunar event sites indicated by stars
[After Middlehurst and Moore, 1967, Science 155, 449.]

108 IS SOMEONE ON THE MOON?

Frontispiece-Topographical distribution of reported lunar event sites indicated by stars [After Middlehurst and Moore, 1967, Science 755, 449.]

IV

CHRONOLOGICAL CATALOG OF REPORTED LUNAR EVENTS

by

Barbara M. Middlehurst,[*] Jaylee M. Burley, Patrick Moore,[†] and Barbara L. Welther[‡]

INTRODUCTION

A catalog of reports of lunar events, or temporary changes on the moon, has been compiled based on literature covering more than four centuries. In the majority of cases the original reference has been consulted; secondary sources such as the new (1964) edition of Houzeau and Lancaster's *Bibliographie Général d'Astronomie* and the *Astronomischer Jahresbericht* were also used. Each entry includes a brief description and date of the observation, the name of the observer(s), where these are known, and the reference. The purpose of this catalog is to provide a listing of historical and modern records that may be useful in investigations of possible activity on the moon.

DESCRIPTION OF THE CATALOG

A lunar event is defined here as a temporary change, other than that due merely to conditions of illumination, in the appearance of a lunar feature involving a limited area, generally a few kilometers in dimension. Reports of observations of temporary bright spots, as well as veils, obscurations, and brightening of the floors of craters and other small areas have been included. No reports of apparently long-term changes are given; many of these have been reported for sites such as Messier, Linné, and Bartlett, but in most cases, the evidence is not conclusive for real changes, as it involved conflicting reports of the craters' appearances over periods of years, rather than changes actually in progress.

The catalog contains all information available to us through October 1967; many of the reports listed are taken from publications that are not now generally available. Column 1 gives a running number, column 2 the date of the occurrence, Gregorian except for the first entry which predates

[*]Lunar and Planetary Laboratory, University of Arizona, Tucson, Arizona.
[†]Armagh Planetarium, Armagh, Northern Ireland.
[‡]Smithsonian Astrophysical Observatory, Cambridge, Massachusetts.

1

CHRONOLOGICAL CATALOG OF REPORTED LUNAR EVENTS

by
Barbara M. Middlehurst, * Jaylee M. Burley, Patrick Moore/
and Barbara L. Welther*

INTRODUCTION

A catalog of reports of lunar events, or temporary changes on the moon, has been compiled based on literature covering more than four centuries. In the majority of cases the original reference has been consulted; secondary sources such as the new (1964) edition of Houzeau and Lan- caster's Bibliographie General d'Astronomie and the Astronomischer Jahresbericht were also used. Each entry includes a brief description and date of the observation, the name of the observers), where these are known, and the reference. The purpose of this catalog is to provide a listing of historical and modern records that may be useful in investigations of possible activity on the moon.

DESCRIPTION OF THE CATALOG

A lunar event is defined here as a temporary change, other than that due merely to conditions of illumination, in the appearance of a lunar feature involving a limited area, generally a few kilometers in dimension. Reports of observations of temporary bright spots, as well as veils, obscurations, and brightening of the floors of craters and other small areas have been included. No reports of apparently long-term changes are given; many of these have been reported for sites such as Messier, Linne, and Bartlett, but in most cases, the evidence is not conclusive for real changes, as it involved conflicting reports of the craters' appearances over periods of years, rather than changes actually in progress.

The catalog contains all information available to us through October 1967; many of the reports listed are taken from publications that are not now generally available. Column 1 gives a running number, column 2 the date of the occurrence, Gregorian except for the first entry which predates

•Lunar and Planetary Laboratory, University of Arizona, Tucson, Arizona. tArmagh Planetarium, Armagh, Northern Ireland.
tSmithsonian Asttophysical Observatory, Cambridge, Massachusetts.

the use of the Gregorian calendar* and the time at 0° longitude except where otherwise noted, column 3 the site and duration of the event, column 4 a short description of the phenomenon, column 5 the observer, and column 6 the reference. The references are given alphabetically following the catalog. Where permanent records (e.g., photographs, spectra, or photometric or spectrometric records) exist, a footnote is given.

Due to the form of the data presentation the maximum duration of the changes as listed covers a few hours only; nevertheless, it may not properly represent the total period of activity in the site. Many cases of reports for the same site on consecutive or nearly consecutive nights are given, and weather and other factors may have limited the observing period within a single night.

Throughout the catalog the use of the terms "east" and "west" follows the convention adopted by the International Astronomical Union (IAU) in 1961 in which the classical, or astronomical, "east" was changed to the astronautical "west", which is in agreement with ordinary terrestrial mapping with east at right and west at left.

As far as possible, we eliminated reports of events that, for one reason or another (e.g., possibly because of special lighting effects, multiple reflections, and changes of appearance caused by libration), are considered to be spurious. Reports of this type are discussed in the following section. In a large number of the historical cases, the high stature of the observer as a scientist inspires confidence in the reliability of the report and, for the rest, we saw no reason to dismiss the observation except in the cases listed in the next section. Almost certainly some doubtful cases remain listed in the catalog. However, their distribution with respect to almost any non-observational lunar variable is probably random, and we believe that statistically they are unimportant.

The fraction of past events which is recorded in the available literature is difficult to assess. Over the years, interest in lunar matters, and particularly in changes and events, has waxed and waned. Wars have intervened, and bad weather cycles have undoubtedly reduced the amount of observing at times. The number of observed lunar events is influenced by many other factors, such as the light-gathering power and resolution of the telescope used, the amount of time devoted to observation, and the skill and experience of the observers. It is notable that a marked increase in the frequency of the reports occurs from 1783 to 1800 following Herschel's observations of "lunar volcanoes" on May 4, 1783. This increase is almost certainly due to the interest generated among astronomers in England, France, and Germany. The gap between 1800 and 1821 correlates with unrest in Europe where most astronomers of that period lived. In 1813 the Napoleonic armies returning from Moscow overran and destroyed Schröter's observatory, home, and many of his later manuscripts. The time was a difficult one for science, and few advances in astronomy were made.

Reports of dark-side events are more frequent among the earlier observations, when the light-gathering power of most telescopes was relatively small and the field often included the image of

* Adopted in 1582 in Catholic countries, but not until 1752 in England and her colonies, and in 1923 in Russia and other Eastern Orthodox countries.

the use of the Gregorian calendar* and the time at 0° longitude except where otherwise noted, column 3 the site and duration of the event, column 4 a short description of the phenomenon, column 5 the observer, and column 6 the reference. The references are given alphabetically following the catalog. Where permanent records (e.g., photographs, spectra, or photometric or spectrometric records) exist, a footnote is given.

Due to the form of the data presentation the maximum duration of the changes as listed covers a few hours only; nevertheless, it may not properly represent the total period of activity in the site. Manycasesofreportsforthesamesiteonconsecutiveornearlyconsecutivenightsare given, and weather and other factors may have limited the observing period within a single night.

Throughout the catalog the use of the terms "east" and "west" follows the convention adopted by the International Astronomical Union (IAU) in 1961 in which the classical, or astronomical, "east" was changed to the astronautical "west", which agrees with ordinary terrestrial mapping with east at right and west at left.

As far as possible, we eliminated reports of events that, for one reason or another (e.g., possibly because of special lighting effects, multiple reflections, and changes of appearance caused by libration), are considered to be spurious. Reports of this type are discussed in the following section. In a large number of the historical cases, the high stature of the observer as a scientist inspires confidence in the reliability of the report and, for the rest, we saw no reason to dismiss the observation except in the cases listed in the next section. Almost certainly some doubtful cases remain listed in the catalog. However, their distribution with respect to almost any non- observational lunar variable is probably random, and we believe that statistically they are unimportant.

The fraction of past events which is recorded in the available literature is difficult to assess. Over the years, interest in lunar matters, and particularly in changes and events, has waxed and waned. Wars have intervened, and bad weather cycles have undoubtedly reduced the amount of observing at times. The number of observed lunar events is influenced by many other factors, such as the light-gathering power and resolution of the telescope used, the amount of time devoted to observation, and the skill and experience of the observers. It is notable that a marked increase in the frequency of the reports occurs from 1783 to 1800 following Herschel's observations of "lunar volcanoes" on May 4, 1783. This increase is almost certainly due to the interest generated among astronomers in England, France, and Germany. The gap between 1800 and 1821 correlates with unrest in Europe where most astronomers of that period lived. In1813theNapoleonicarmies returning from Moscow overran and destroyed Schroter's observatory, home, and many of his later manuscripts. The time was a difficult one for science, and few advances in astronomy were made.

Reports of dark-side events are more frequent among the earlier observations, when the light- gathering power of most telescopes was relatively small and the field often included the image of

"Adopted in 1582 in Catholic countries, but not until 1752 in England and net colonies, and in 1923 in Russia and other Eastern Orthodox countries.

the whole moon. Operation Moon Blink (described elsewhere, e.g., Association of Lunar and Planetary Observers (ALPO) reports) and similar undertakings in other countries helped increase the frequency of reports of lunar events during the last few years. The frontispiece shows the topographical distribution of sites of reported lunar events.

REPORTS OMITTED FROM THE CATALOG

We attempted to eliminate all doubtful reports from this catalog. Less than full realization by the observers of the effects of changing conditions of illumination and other factors may have resulted in erroneous reports. Hazards of illumination include earthshine (strongest during the first and last three days of a lunation), sunshine on peaks just beyond the terminator, differences in albedo and color in small regions, and multiple reflections from crater walls. Careless reporting has been discovered in one case only (Hammes 1878, see below).

The following records are reports in which special appearances may be due to unusual lighting conditions or other temporary effects external to the moon, or which are unacceptable for other reasons. These reports are not included in the catalog.

1789 July 30. J. H. Schröter (1791, *Selenotopographische Fragmente*) "soon after sunrise" saw a kind of ferment on the floor of Plato which clearly resembled a kind of twilight.

1856 April 8, and 1860 April 24. J. Schmidt (1879, *Vierteljahrschrift für Astronomie, 14*, 265) noted weak glows in the crater Boussingault, but he doubted that these were more than sunlight on the walls re-reflected from the floor.

1878 November 12, 8:30 local time. John Hammes and friends in Iowa reported seeing a lunar "volcano." Correspondence in *Scientific American* (Dec. 21, 1878, *39*, 385) includes drawings, an identification by Admiral Rogers of the supposed location, and a certification of John Hammes' respectability and good standing by the Mayor and three other citizens of Koekuk, Iowa. On investigation, it became clear that some of Hammes' details were incorrect, and since his drawings showed such poor detail, the site identification is questionable.

1899 August 29. P. Fauth (1899, *Astr. Nach.*, 151, 219) noted that the inner parts of Copernicus glowed in weak phosphorescent light though not directly lighted by the sun. The observer noted, however, that the effect was probably due to multiple reflection, as the sun was then shining on the walls of the crater.

1909 January 24 and 25. Krebs (1909, *Astr. Nach.*, 181, 45) and Nicolls noted that the non-illuminated part of the moon glowed red. These observations may have been due to special effects in the earth's atmosphere. Some eclipse reports originally included have been omitted from the list for similar reasons. Only where the observers described clearly bounded bright areas or rapid changes in brightness have eclipse observations been listed.

the whole moon. Operation Moon Blink (described elsewhere, e.g., Association of Lunar and Planetary Observers (ALPO) reports) and similar undertakings in other countries helped increase the frequency of reports of lunar events during the last few years. The frontispiece shows the topographical distribution of sites of reported lunar events.

REPORTS OMITTED FROM THE CATALOG

We attempted to eliminate all doubtful reports from this catalog. Less than full realization by the observers of the effects of changing conditions of illumination and other factors may have resulted in erroneous reports. Hazards of illumination include earthshine (strongest during the first and last three days of a lunation), sunshine on peaks just beyond the terminator, differences in albedo and color in small regions, and multiple reflections from crater walls. Careless re- porting has been discovered in one case only (Hammes 1878, see below).

The following records are reports in which special appearances may be due to unusual lighting conditions or other temporary effects external to the moon, or which are unacceptable for other reasons. These reports are not included in the catalog.

1789 July 30. J. H. Schroter (1791, Selenotopographische Fragmente) "soon after sunrise" saw a kind of ferment on the floor of Plato which clearly resembled a kind of twilight.

1856 April 8, and 1860 April 24. J. Schmidt (1879, Vierteljahrschrift fiir Astronomie, 14, 265) noted weak glows in the crater Boussingault, but he doubted that these were more than sunlight on the walls re- reflected from the floor.

1878 November 12, 8:30 local time. John Hammes and friends in Iowa reported seeing a lunar "volcano." Correspondence in Scientific American (Dec. 21, 1878, 39, 385) includes drawings, an identification by Admiral Rogers of the supposed location, and a certification of John Hammes' respectability and good standing by the Mayor and three other citizens of Keokuk, Iowa. On investigation, it became clear that some of Hammes' details were incorrect, and since his drawings showed such poor detail, the site identification is questionable.

1899 August 29. P. Fauth (1899, Astr. Nach., 151, 219) noted that the inner parts of Copernicus glowed in weak phosphorescent light though not directly lighted by the sun. The observer noted, however, that the effect was probably due to multiple reflection, as the sun was then shining on the walls of the crater.

1909 January 24 and 25. Krebs (1909, Astr. Nach., 181, 45) and Nicolis noted that the non-illuminated part of the moon glowed red. These observations may have been due to special effects in the earth's atmosphere. Some eclipse reports originally included have been omitted from the list for similar reasons. Only where the observers described clearly bounded bright areas or rapid changes in brightness have eclipse observations been listed.

1964 - . Where the observations record progressive changes (on a number of occasions) by a succession of observers, apparently without adequate checks on subjectiveness, we felt sufficient doubt of the reality of a lunar event to omit the report.

In spite of the care taken, we may have wrongly included (or excluded) a number of items, but we believe that the total of these is quite small. For additional evidence in regard to the list of reported events, the following critical discussions and references are given:

Burley, J. M., and Middlehurst, B. M., 1966, "Apparent Lunar Activity: Historical Review," *Proc. Nat. Acad. Sci.*, 55, No. 5, 1007-1011.

Chapman, W. B., 1967, "Tidal Influences at the Lunar Crater Aristarchus," *J. Geophys. Res.*, 72, No. 24, 6293-6298.

Middlehurst, B. M., and Moore, P. A., 1967, "Topographical Distribution of Lunar Transient Phenomena," *Science*, 155, No. 3761, 449-451.

Middlehurst, B. M., 1967, "An Analysis of Lunar Events," *Reviews of Geophysics*, 5, No. 2, 173-189.

Middlehurst, B. M., 1967, "A Note on Lunar Transient Phenomena," *Icarus*, 6, No. 1, 140-142.

ACKNOWLEDGMENTS

We wish to record with gratitude help given by Miss C. Botley and others in locating many old journals and the contributions of data by Drs. J. Larink, J. A. O'Keefe, P. Treanor, Mrs. W. Cameron and many others. Mr. E. Whitaker kindly checked the evaluation of lighting conditions. Thanks are due for the kindness that made many items freely available for checking, especially in the libraries of Harvard Observatory, Kitt Peak National Observatory, and the Royal Astronomical Society. The support of the National Science Foundation through Grants GP-5940 and GP-6709 is gratefully acknowledged by B. M. Middlehurst. Mrs. Betty Fink assisted in the library search, in checking references and in preparing the manuscript for publication.

1964 - Where the observations record progressive changes (on a number of occasions) by a succession of observers, apparently without adequate checks on subjectiveness, we felt sufficient doubt of the reality of a lunar event to omit the report.

In spite of the care taken, we may have wrongly included (or excluded) a number of items, but we believe that the total of these is quite small. For additional evidence in regard to the list of reported events, the following critical discussions and references are given:

Burley, J. M., and Middlehurst, B. M., 1966, "Apparent Lunar Activity: Historical Review," Proc. Nat. Acad. Sci., 55, No. 5, 1007-1011.

Chapman, W. B., 1967, "Tidal Influences at the Lunar Crater Aristarchus," J. Geophys. Res., 72, No. 24, 6293-6298.

Middlehurst, B. M., and Moore, P. A., 1967, "Topographical Distribution of Lunar Transient Phenomena," Science, 155, No. 3761, 449-451.

Middlehurst, B. M., 1967, "An Analysis of Lunar Events," Reviews of Geophysics, 5, No. 2, 173-189.

Middlehurst, B. M., 1967, "A Note on Lunar Transient Phenomena," Icarus, 6, No. 1, 140-142.

ACKNOWLEDGMENTS

We wish to record with gratitude help given by Miss C. Botley and others in locating many old journals and the contributions of data by Drs. J. Larink, J. A. O'Keefe, P. Treanor, Mrs. W. Cameron and many others. Mr. E. Whitaker kindly checked the evaluation of lighting conditions. Thanks are due for the kindness that made many items freely available for checking, especially in the libraries of Harvard Observatory, Kitt Peak National Observatory, and the Royal Astronomica lSociety. The support of the National Science Foundation through Grants GP-5940andGP-6709 is gratefully acknowledged by B. M. Middlehurst. Mrs. Betty Fink assisted in the library search, in checking references and in preparing the manuscript for publication.

CHRONOLOGICAL CATALOG OF REPORTED LUNAR EVENTS[1]

No.	Date and Time	Feature or Location, Duration	Description	Observer	Reference
1	1540 Nov 26, ~05ʰ00ᵐ	Region of Calippus[2]	Starlike appearance on dark side.	Observers at Worms	Bess 1911
2	1587 Mar 5[3]	Dark side	"A sterre is seen in the bkacke of the moone upon the thinnis of Marche, whereof many men merveiled, and not without cause, for it stode directly betwene the pointes of her hornes, the moone being changed, not passing 5 or 6 daies before."	Anonymous	Harrison 1876; Lowes 1927
3	1650	Aristarchus	"Red hill." More Porphyrites.	Hevelius	B.A.A. Lunar Sec. Circ. 1967, 2, No. 8
4	1668 Nov 26[3]	Dark side	Bright starlike point.	Several New Englanders	Josselyn 1675; Mather 1714; Lowes 1927
5	1671 Oct 21	Pitatus			Bode 1792a; Lalande 1792 (1966)
6	1671 Nov 12	Pitatus	Small whitish cloud.	D. Cassini	Bode 1792a; Lalande 1792 (1966)
7	1672 Feb 3	Mare Crisium	Nebulous appearance.	D. Cassini	Bode 1792a; Lalande 1792 (1966)
8	1673 Oct 18	Pitatus	White spot.	D. Cassini	Bode 1792a; Lalande 1792 (1966)
9	1685 Dec 10, 22ʰ25ᵐ	Plato	Reddish streak on crater floor seen during eclipse thereof.	Bianchini	Bianchini 1686; Slade 1965
10	1706 May 12		Three sparkling spots.		Bode 1792a
11	1715 May 3, ~09ʰ36ᵐ		"Lightning" on the face of the moon. De Louville explained this as storms. Halley reference uses Old Style date.	Louville, Halley	Louville 1715; Halley 1715; Schröter 1791; Boutreau 1882; Fontenau and Launcaster 1962 ed.

No.	Date and Time	Feature of Location; Duration	Description	Observer	Reference
12	1725 Aug 16	Plato	A track of ruddy light, like a beam, crossing the middle of the obscure (shadowed) area (crater in darkness).	Bianchini	Hosp., Phos., Chapman, 1722; Sirius 1887; Wilkins 1955
13	1738 Aug 4, 16ʰ 31ᵐ		During solar eclipse, appearance like lightning on the face of the moon. (Partial eclipse.)	Friend of Weidler	Phil. Trans. 1728
14	1751 Apr 22	Plato	Yellow streak of light across crater floor while crater was in darkness.	Short, Stephens, Harris	Sirius 1887
15	1772 Oct 11, 17ʰ 0ᵐ		Bright spot on disk of fully eclipsed moon.	Beccaria's nephew and niece	Beccaria 1781; Klado 1965
16	1774 Jul 25	Mare Crisium	Four bright spots. Peculiar behavior of terminator.	Eysenhard	Webb 1962 ed., pp. 106–107
17	1778 Jun 24, 15ʰ 55ᵐ	½ min	During solar eclipse, observed spot near lunar limb almost as bright as sun.	Ulloa	Ulloa 1779, 1780; Houzeau and Lancaster 1964 ed.; Klado 1965
18	1783 Mar 18 or Sep 16		Moving gleam around middle of disk during lunar eclipse.	Messier	Lhts 1893; Pop. Astr. 1894–95
19	1783 May	Near Aristarchus	Bright points seen during observation of star occultation.	W. Herschel	Schröter 1791
20	1783 May 4	Aristarchus, vicinity	Red spot, 3ʰ mag. diameter <3".	W. Herschel, Mrs. Lind	Herschel 1912
21	1784	Aristarchus	Nebulous bright spot of light.	Schröter	Schröter 1791
22	1785	Aristarchus	Nebulous bright spot of light.	Schröter	Schröter 1791
23	1786 Dec 24	Aristarchus	Extraordinarily bright.	Schröter	Schröter 1791
24	1787 May	Dark side	Three bright spots.	W. Herschel	Schröter 1791
25	1787 Apr 19	Dark side	Three "volcanoes." The brightest, 3°57′3 from N limb, the other two much farther toward the center of the moon.	W. Herschel	Herschel 1787, 1912
26	1787 Apr 20	Dark side	Brightest "volcano" even brighter and at least 3 mi in diameter.	W. Herschel	Herschel 1787, 1912
27	1787 May 19–20	Aristarchus	Extraordinarily bright.	von Brühl	Bode 1790; Schröter 1791; Herschel 1912

No.	Date and Time	Feature or Location; Duration	Description	Observer	Reference
28	1787 May 22	Helicon	Bright spot on dark side.	Villeneuve	Lalande 1792 (1966)
29	1788 Jan 11	Near Plato		Observers in Mannheim	Schröter 1791
30	1788 Mar 9–10	Dark side	Bright spot.	Schröter	Schröter 1791
31	1788 Mar 13	Riccioli	Bright spot.	Schröter	Schröter 1791
32	1788 Mar 13	Helicon	Lunar volcano like 6th mag. star.	Nouet	Schröter 1791; Bode 1792a; Lalande 1792 (1966)
33	1788 Apr 9	Aristarchus; 1 hr	Extraordinarily bright.	Bode	Bode 1792b
34	1788 Apr 9–11	Aristarchus	Bright spot 26" N of crater rim.	Schröter, Bode	Schröter 1788, 1791, 1792a, 1792b
35	1788 May 8		Bright spots.	Mechain	Lalande 1792 (1966)
36	1788 May 8–9		Bright spots.	Bode	Bode 1792b
37	1788 Aug 27		Bright spot.	Schröter	Schröter 1791
38	1788 Sep 26, 4:25 am	N edge of Mare Crisium	Small nebulous bright spot.	Schröter	Rozier 1788, 1792; Schröter 1791
39	1788 Sep 26	1°18' SE of Plato; 15 min	Whitish bright spot shining somewhat hazily and 4" to 5" in diameter, 5th mag, SE of Plato in bright mountainous region bounding Mare Imbrium.	Schröter	Schröter 1789, 1792a, 1792b; Sirius 1888
40	1788 Sep 26	Near Aristarchus; 30 min	Bright spot 26" N of main crater.	Schröter	Rozier 1788, 1792; Schröter 1791
41	1788 Dec 2, 3:35 am	Aristarchus	Extraordinarily bright, like star.	Schröter	Schröter 1791
42	1788 Dec 31	Plato	Bright area, like than white cloud.	Schröter	Klein, Woch. für Astr.; Sirius 1878
43	1788	Aristarchus	Brilliant spots.	Bode	Bode 1792b, Houzeau and Lancaster 1964 ed.
44	1789 Jan 10		Lunar volcano.	Seyffer	Seyffer 1789; Houzeau and Lancaster 1964 ed.

No.	Date and Time	Feature or Location, Caution	Description	Observer	Reference
45	1788 Mar 29-30	Grimaldi, also near Bucolid	Two flickering spots on E edge of Grimaldi, and near fireside on dark side of moon; a bright spot.	Schröter	Schröter 1784, 1791; Houzeau and Lancaster 1964 ed.
46	1788 May 29-31	Aristarchus	Nebulous bright area.	Schröter	Schröter 1791
47	1788 Mar	Near Aristarchus	Brilliant spots near Aristarchus; luminous spots on dark side.	Bode	Bode 1788-89, 1789, 1790; Houzeau and Lancaster 1964 ed.
48	1788 Apr	Near Aristarchus	Brilliant spots near Aristarchus; luminous spots on dark side.	Bode	Bode 1788-89, 1789, 1790; Houzeau and Lancaster 1964 ed.
49	1788 May	Near Aristarchus	Brilliant spots near Aristarchus; luminous spots on dark side.	Bode	Bode 1788-89, 1789, 1790; Houzeau and Lancaster 1964 ed.
50	1788 Sep 26	Mont Blanc; 15 min	Small speck of light at foot of mountain, like 5th mag star.	Schröter	Pickering 1962; Webb 1962 ed., p. 113
51	1790 Jan 17	Aristarchus region	Small, hazy spot of light.	Schröter	Schröter 1791
52	1790 Feb 15-18	Aristarchus region	Small, hazy spot of light.	Schröter	Schröter 1791
53	1790 Mar 19	Aristarchus region	Small, hazy spot of light.	Schröter	Schröter 1791
54	1790 Oct 22		During total eclipse, Herschel saw at least 150 small, round, bright, red luminous points. (1Md=eclipse, lunar, Oct 22, 09h41m.)	W. Herschel	Herschel 1912 ed.; Klein 1865
55	1792 Feb 24		Cusps of moon showed signs of atmosphere.	Schröter	Webb 1962 ed., p. 92
56	1792		Many occasions; special appearance.	Bode	Bode 1792a
57	1792	Dark side	Brilliant spots.	Schröter	Schröter 1792a, 1792b
58	1794 Mar 7	Dark side; 15 min	Appearance of light like a star seen in dark part of the moon.	W. Wilkins, Stretton	Wilkins 1794; Stretton 1794; Masielyne 1795; Moore 1953; Houzeau and Lancaster 1964 ed.
59	1797 Mar 2	Promontorium Heraclides, vicinity	"Observations of a volcano on the moon."	Caroché	Caroché 1799; Houzeau and Lancaster 1964 ed.
60	1797 Jul 3	Mare Vaporum	Vapors resembling mountain.	Schröter, Others	Klein 1879

No.	Date and Time	Feature or Location; Duration	Description	Observer	Reference
61	1799	Dark side	Bright spots on dark side, seen during five different lunations.	Piazzi	Piazzi 1800; Rozeau and Lancaster 1964 ed.; Tresauw and O'Connell 1965
62	1820 Oct 1?	S of Sinus Iridum	Brilliant spots in Mare Imbrium S of Sinus Iridum.	Lathmer	Lathmer 1824
63	1821 Feb 5-6	Aristarchus, vicinity	Luminous appearance on dark side; 6th to 7th mag, 3" to 4" diameter.	Kater, Olbers, Browne	Kater 1821; Olbers 1822, 1824; Gauss 1874; Rozeau and Lancaster 1964 ed.
64	1821 Apr ?	Posidonius	Appeared without shadow.	Gruithuisen	Webb 1962 ed., p. 110
65	1821 May 4-5	Aristarchus, vicinity	Bright spot on dark side, <1" diameter.	Ward, Baily	Ward 1822; Baily 1822
66	1821 Jul 25	Dark side	Brilliant flashing spots.	Gruithuisen	Gruithuisen 1825
67	1821 Nov 28, ~20h00m	Dark side	Variable bright spot like 6th mag star.	Fallows	Fallows 1822
68	1822 Jan 27	Aristarchus, vicinity	Bright spot like 5th mag star.	F. G. W. Struve	Struve 1825
69	1822 Jun 22-23	Aristarchus	"Volcanoes" on the moon; several occasions.	Bippell	Bippell 1822
70	1822		Lunar "volcano."	Tlauguegues	Tlauguegues 1822
71	1822			Zach	Zach 1822
72	1824 May 1	Near Aristarchus	Blinding light, 9th to 10th mag on dark side.	Göbel	Göbel 1826
73	1824 Oct 18	Aristarchus, vicinity	Mingling of all kinds of colors in small spots in the W and NW of Aristarchus.	Gruithuisen	Gruithuisen 1825; Pauth 1899
74	1824 Oct 29, 03h00m	Dark side, Mare Nubium	Bright area 100 x 20 km.	Gruithuisen	Flammarion 1884; Arcade 1962
75	1825 Dec 8	Plato	Bright flock in SE part of crater.	Gruithuisen	Sirius 1879
76	1825 Apr 8	Plato	W part of crater brighter than E part.	Gruithuisen	Sirius 1879
77	1825 Apr 22	Aristarchus and vicinity	Periodic illumination.	Argelander, Göbel	Argelander 1826; Göbel 1826

No.	Date and Time	Feature or Location; Duration	Description	Observer	Reference
78	1825 Dec 1, 23h45m	Ptolemaeus	Bright spot.	Schroter	Sel. J. 1840
79	1826 Apr 12, 20h06m	Mare Crisium	Black moving haze or cloud.	Emmett	Emmett 1826; Capron 1879
80	1826 Apr 15, 20h06m	Mare Crisium, 1 hr	Cloud lens intense.	Emmett	Capron 1879
81	1832 Jul 4	Mare Crisium	Specklet with minute dots and streaks of light.	T. W. Webb	Astr. Reg. 1882; Webb 1962 ed., p. 105
82	1832 Dec 25	Aristarchus, vicinity	Bright spot.	C. P. Smyth	Smyth 1836
83	1835 Dec 22, 18h30m	Near Aristarchus	Bright spot, 8th to 10th mag.	C. P. Smyth	Smyth 1836
84	1836 Feb 12	Messier	Two straight lines of light; a band between, covered with luminous points.	Gruithuisen	Sci. Amer. Supp. Vol. 7
85	1839 Jun 24	Grimaldi	Smoky-gray mist.	Gruithuisen	B.A.A. Mem. 1895
86	1839 Jul 7	South Pole	Twilight.	Gruithuisen	B.A.A. Mem. 1895
87	1839 Jul 19	Schroter	Dark mist.	Gruithuisen	B.A.A. Mem. 1895
88	1842 Jul 8, 07h02m	Peak S of Alps	During solar eclipse, moon's disk occasionally crossed by bright streaks.		Wullerstorff 1846; Zanoiesecki 1846
89	1843 Jul 4		On terminator saw an unusually bright spot that glowed like a fixed star.	Gerling	Gerling 1845; Sirius 1889
90	1844 Apr 25	SW of Pico	A bluish glimmering patch of light, not quite within the night side of the moon.	J. Schmidt	Sel. J. 1878
91	1847 Mar 18, 19	Dark side	Large luminous spots on dark side.	Rankin, Chevalier	Rankin 1847; Houzeau and Lancaster 1964 ed.
92	1847 Dec 11, 18h00m	Teneriffe Mts.	A bright spot about 1/4-ring diam of Saturn was perceived which, though it varied in intensity like an intermittent light, was at all times visible (dark side).	Hodgson	Hodgson 1848
93	1848 Mar 19, 21h42m		During eclipse, rapid changes in red color. (Lunar eclipse.)	Gorjan	M. N. 1847–48; Link 1865

No.	Date and Time	Feature or Location; Duration	Description	Observer	Reference
94	1849 Feb 11	Posidonius	Without normal shadow.	J. Schmidt	Webb 1962 ed., p. 110
95	1854 Dec 27	Teneriffe Mts. (near Plato); 5 hr	Two luminous fiery spots on bright side, "...an appearance I had never seen before on the surface of the moon though I have observed her often these last 40 years.... It appeared to me from the brightness of the light and the contrast of colour, to be two active volcanoes or 2 mouths of one in action."	Hart	Hart 1855
96	1855 Jun 20		Traces of twilight seen. Webb gives low weight to observation "for want of better optical means."	Webb	Webb 1962 ed., p. 97
97	1862 Jun 15, 06^h 19^m		"During [lunar] eclipse, the E [AA':W] side dark brick red and something seemed to oscillate before it." At mid-eclipse on the S side, "a very small meniscus was seen nearly the color of the uneclipsed moon."		Main 1865
98	1864 May 5 and Oct 15	Mare Crisium, E of Picard	Bright cloud.	Ingall	Ingall 1864
99	1864		Bright spot.	Birt	Birt 1864
100	1865 Jan 1	SE of Plato; 30 min	Bright spot like 4th mag star slightly out of focus. Bright speck remained changeless for 30 min, and its light was steady.	Grover	Grover 1866; Webb 1962 ed., p. 114
101	1865 Apr 30	Mare Crisium, E of Picard	Point of light like star. Whole of Mare Crisium intersected with bright veins, mixed with bright spots of light. Aperture 4-1/2 in., 4 hr before full moon.	Ingall	Astr. Reg. 1866
102	1865 Sep 5	Mare Crisium, E of Picard	Point of light like star, with misty cloud.	Ingall	Astr. Reg. 1866
103	1865 Nov 21	Carlini; 1 hr 30 min	Dark side, distinct bright speck like 8th mag star.	Williams and two others	Webb 1962 ed., p. 125

No.	Date and Time	Feature or Location, Duration	Description	Observer	Reference
104	1865	Mare Crisium	Dots and streaks of light.	Slack, Ingall	Webb 1962 ed., p. 108
105	1865 Jun 10	Aristarchus	Starlike light.	Tempel	Denning, Tel. Work, p. 121
106	1865 Jan 11–18	Aristarchus, vicinity	Reddish-yellow.	Tempel	Tempel 1867
107	1866	Dark side	Bright spots.	Hodgson	Hodgson 1866
108	1867 Apr 9, 19h 29m – 23h 06m	Aristarchus, vicinity 1 hr 30 min	Bright spot on dark side, 7th mag, becoming fainter after 26h15m UT.	Elger	Elger 1868
109	1867 Apr 12, 27h 29m – 28h 30m	Aristarchus, vicinity 1 hr	Bright spot on dark side, 7th mag.	Elger	Webb 1962 ed., p. 53
110	1867 May 6–7	Aristarchus; at least several hours each night	Left side of crater, very bright luminous point, appearing like a volcano.	Flammarion	Flammarion 1884
111	1867 May 7	Aristarchus, vicinity	Reddish-yellow, heaven-like light.	Tempel	Tempel 1867; Astr. Reg. 1868
112	1867 Jun 10	Subpicus Gallus	Three blackish spots.	Dawes	The Student Vol. 1
113	1867	Dark side	Bright spots.	W. O. Williams	Williams 1867
114	1870 May 13	Plato	Bright spot, extraordinary display.	Pratt, Elger	Rept. Brit. Assn. 1871
115	1870		White spots on the moon; "lightning."	Birt	Birt 1870
116	1870	Godin	Purplish haze illuminating floor of crater, still in shadow.	Trouvelot	Trouvelot 1882; Moore 1903
117	1871	Plato	Streak of light across floor while crater in shadow.	Elger	Sirius 1887
118	1871	W of Plato	Fog or mist.	Elger, Nelson	Flammarion 1884
119	1872 Jul 16	Plato	NE portion of floor hazy.	Pratt	Capron 1879
120	1873 Jan 4	Kant	Luminous purplish vapors.	Trouvelot	Trouvelot 1882; Flammarion 1884; Moore 1963

No.	Date and Time	Feature or Location; Duration	Description	Observer	Reference
121	1873 Apr 10	Plato	Under high sun, two faint clouds in W part of crater.	Schmidt	Sirius 1879
122	1873 Nov 1	Plato	Unusual appearance.	Pratt	Capron 1879
123	1874 Jan 1	Plato	Unusual appearance.	Pratt	Capron 1879
124	1877 Feb 20, 03h30m–16h30m	Endymion; 1 hr	Fine line of light like luminous cable drawn W to E across crater.	Trouvelot	Flammarion 1884; l'Astron. 1885
125	1877 Feb 27, 19h19m		Lunar eclipse. Flickering light on lunar surface.	Doena	l'Opin. Nat'ion. 1877
126	1877 Mar 17, 06h45m		Moon's horns showed trace of atmosphere. Moon 2°46' obl (2.75-in. reflector).	Dennett	Eng. Mech. 1882
127	1877 Mar 23	Proclus	Brilliant illumination.	Barrett	Eng. Mech. 1882
128	1877 May 12, 26h30m and May 29, 00h45m	E of Picard	Bright spot.		Eng. Mech. 1882
129	1877 Jun 17, 22h40m	Bessel	Minute point of light (seen with 2.75-in. reflector).	Dennett	Eng. Mech. 1882
130	1877 Jul 29	Plato	S of center of crater, bright streak; disappeared at 2:30 a.m.	Gray	Flammarion 1884
131	1877 Aug 23–24, 23h10m		Lunar eclipse. (1) Unusual spectrum with strong absorption in yellow. (2) Two patches of crimson light of short duration.	(1) Airy (2) Capron, Pratt	(1) Sirius 1879 (2) Capron 1879
132	1878 Feb 2, 08h16m	At limb	Changes in spectrum during solar eclipse suggesting lunar atmosphere.	Observers at Melbourne, Australia	Sirius 1879
133	1878 Mar 10, 19h23m	Mare Crisium	White patch E of Picard badly defined.	Noble	Sel. J. 1879
134	1878 Oct 5, 21h30m	Plato	Faint bright shimmer like thin white cloud.	Klein	Klein, Woch. für Astr.; Sirius 1879
135	1878 Oct 21	3 hr	Half of moon's terminator obliterated.	Hirst	Capron 1879
136	1878 Nov 1	Messier	Obscuration of Messier.	Klein	Pop. Astr. 1902

No.	Date and Time	Feature or Location; Duration	Description	Observer	Reference
137	1878 Nov 9, 21h00m	Plato	Faint but unmistakable white cloud, not seen before.	Klein	Sirius 1879
138	1878 Dec 4	Aerjura, Klein's Object, and the oval spot nearby	"Odd misty look as if vapour were in or about them."	Capron	Capron 1879
139	1878	E of Picard	White patch.	Birt	Eng. Mech. Vol. 28
140	1878	Interior of Tycho	Cloudy appearance.	Birt	Eng. Mech. Vol. 28
141	1880 Jan 18	Whole of Mare Nectaris	Foggy. Fog extended into the floor of Fracastorius. Gruithuisen said that the seeing was unsatisfactory.	Gaudibert	Gaudibert 1880
142	1881 Feb 3, 19h00m	Aristarchus (on dark side, limb seen)	Very bright (~8.0 mag star) with pulsations.	"Gamma"	Sirius 1881
143	1881? Jul 4, 06h39m	Aristarchus region	"Two pyramidal luminous protuberances appeared on the moon's limb.... These points were a little darker than the rest of the moon's face. They slowly faded away...."	Several observers	Sci. Amer. 1882
144	1881 Aug 6–7	Aristarchus region	Whole region between Aristarchus and Herodotus and S part of Great Rille (Schröter's Valley) appeared in strong violet light as if covered with fog.	Klein	Klein 1902
145	1881 Dec 3, 17h09m	Aristarchus	During eclipse, Aristarchus was a white spot in the coppery disk and continued so. (Lunar eclipse.)	S. J. Johnson	Johnson 1882; Fisher 1924
146	1882 Jan 28, 17h00m – 17h30m	Endymion; 30 min	Unusual shadow.		Sirius 1882
147	1882 Feb 27, 18h30m – 19h30m and 20h30m – 20h45m	Endymion; 1 hr, and 15 min	Unusual shadow (on Feb 25, the shadow was normal).		Sirius 1882
148	1882 Mar 27, 16h45m	Plato	Floor glassed with milky light.	A. S. Williams	Williams 1882

No.	Date and Time	Feature or Location; Duration	Description	Observer	Reference
149	1882 Apr 24	Near Godin and Agrippa	Shadows blurred and oscillating. Shadows in Aristotelies steady. Intervals between obscurations, ~10 min.	Riehl	Proc. Liverpool Astr. Soc. 1883
150	1882 May 19	Just E of Mare Crisium against Prom. Agarum	Cloud, not less than 100 mi x 40 or 50 mi; no trace seen on May 20.	J. G. Jackson and friends	Eng. Mech. 1882; Strol. Astr. 1966; B.A.A. Lunar Sec. Circ. 1966, 1, No. 8
151	1882 Jul 17	Just E of Mare Crisium, against Prom. Agarum	Feathery mist or cloud.	J. G. Jackson	Strol. Astr. 1966
152	1882 Nov 7, 09h 00m	Dark limb	Line of light around dark limb, attributed to atmosphere, well seen, equally bright throughout length. Age of moon 26.5 days.	Hopkins	Sirius 1884
153	1883 Mar 12, 20h 00m	Dark limb	Line of light (see 1882 Nov 7), well seen.	Hopkins	Sirius 1884
154	1883 Mar 12	Taruntius and environs	Peculiar blurred appearance. Unmistakable variations in the sharpness of the shadows of the ring plain.	Davies	Proc. Liverpool Astr. Soc. 1883; B.A.A. Lunar Sec. Circ. 1966, 1, No. 10
155	1883 May	Edge of Mare Crisium	Light mist or cloud.	J. G. Jackson	Flammarion 1884
156	1883 Nov 5, ~18h 00m	Aristarchus	Very bright (~7.0–8.0 mag star).	"B_"	Sirius 1885
157	1884 Feb 5	Kepler	Illumination in Kepler.	Morales	l'Astron. Vol. 3
158	1884 Oct 4, ~23h 03m	Tycho	During eclipse, bright spot like a star of the 2nd mag. (1 hour eclipse).	Parschlau	Parschlau 1885; Fisher 1924
159	1884 Nov 29, 19h 00m – 21h 00m	Aristarchus: 2 hr	Nebulous at center; elsewhere features well defined.	Hislop	Sirius 1885

No.	Date and Time	Feature or Location; Duration	Description	Observer	Reference
160	1885 Feb 19	Small crater near Hercules	Small crater was dull red with vivid contrast.	Gray	l'Astron. Vol. 4; Knowledge Vol. 7
161	1885 Feb 27	Cassini	Red patches.	Knott	l'Astron. Vol. 4
162	1886 Jan 10	Aristarchus	Starlike light.	Tempel	Pop. Astr. 1892
163	1886 Sep 6	Plato	Streak of light on dark floor of crater in shadow. (6? mm refl.)	Valkoruna	Sirius 1887
164	1887 Feb 1, ~17h00m	Plato	Appearances of light in crater.	Krüger	Sirius 1887
165	1887 Feb 2	La Hire	Intense yellow streak that cast shadows around neighboring features.	Klein	Sirius 1903
166	1888 Jul 15	S edge of Alps on dark side of moon	Yellow light tinged with red from refractor's secondary spectrum. "Lunar volcano"? ~3 mag. star.	Holden	Sirius 1888
167	1888 Nov 29, 17h15m	45 min	A triangular patch of light (seen with 3 1/2-in. refractor and 180X mag).	von Spelsnos and others	Sirius 1888
168	1889 Mar 30	Copernicus	Black spot.	Gaudibert	l'Astron. 1889
169	1889 May 11	Gassendi	Black spot on rim.	Evon Lade	l'Astron. 1889
170	1889 Jun 6, 22h09m	Plato B and D (Schmidt's designation)	Two extremely bright spots (9-in. refractor).	Krüger	Sirius 1889
171	1889 Jul 12, ~20h52m	Aristarchus	During lunar eclipse, brilliance in surrounding gloom was striking.	Krüger	Krüger 1889; Fisher 1924
172	1889 Sep 3	Alpetragius; 30 min	"Central peak, its shadow and all the floor seem to be seen through haze."	Barnard	Barnard 1892
173	1889 Sep 13	Pitatus	White spot over central peak.	Thury	Thury 1889, 1890
174	1889 Oct 3-4	Alpetragius	Hazy.	Barnard	Barnard 1892
175	1890 Oct 3, ~22h00m	Posidonius	Unusual shadow.	Mellor	Sirius 1890
176	1891 May 23, 18h26m	Aristarchus region	Lunar eclipse, half hour before end of totality, Aristarchus and region immediately N of it became conspicuous and increased in brightness from that time on.	W. E. Jackson	Jackson 1890-91; Fisher 1924

No.	Date and Time	Feature or Location; Duration	Description	Observer	Reference
177	1891 Sep 16	Schröter's Valley	"Dense clouds of white vapour were apparently arising from its bottom and pouring over its SE [AU=SW] wall in the direction of Herodotus."	W. H. Pickering	Pickering 1903
178	1891 Sep 17, 18, 23, 25	Schröter's Valley	Apparent volcanic activity.	W. H. Pickering	Pickering 1903
179	1891 Oct 14	Schröter's Valley	Apparent volcanic activity.	W. H. Pickering	Pickering 1903
180	1891 Nov 7	Aristarchus	Very distinct luminous point.	d'Arrest	l'Astron. Vol. 11
181	1892 Mar 31	Thales	Pale luminous haze.	Barnard	Barnard 1892
182	1892 May 16	Schröter's Valley	Apparent volcanic activity.	W. H. Pickering	Pickering 1903
183	1892 May 11, −22:52″		During partial lunar eclipse, extension of earth's shadow beyond the cusps.		Sirius 1892
184	1893 Jan 30	Schröter's Valley	Apparent volcanic activity.	W. H. Pickering	Pickering 1903
185	1893 Apr 1		Shaft of light.	de Meraes	l'Astron. Vol. 13
186	1894 Feb 23	Henke (now Daniell) and N wall of Posidonius	Strong brownish-red coppery hue in Henke and also on N wall of Posidonius.	Krüger	Sirius 1895
187	1895 Mar 21, 05h 45m	Plato, (1)–12–14 min	During lunar eclipse, very striking color in SE quadrant.	Foulkes	B.A.A. Mem. 1895
188	1895 May 2, (1) 20h 45m (2) 23h 38m		(1) Streak of light, (2) Bright parallel bands in center.	(1) Brenner, (2) Fauth	(1) Sirius 1895, 1897, (2) Sirius 1896, 1897
189	1895 Sep 25		Shaft of light.	Osborne	l'Astron. Vol. 13
190	1896	Macrobius	Penumbral fringe to shadow.	Goodacre	Firsoff 1962 ed., p. 90
191	1897 Jan 14	Schröter's Valley	Apparent volcanic activity.	W. H. Pickering	Pickering 1903
192	1897 Sep 24, 23h 09m	Aristarchus	Glimmering streaks.	Molesworth	Goodacre 1931
193	1897 Oct 4, 10, 13, 5	Schröter's Valley	Apparent volcanic activity.	W. H. Pickering	Pickering 1903
194	1897 Dec 9	Wm. Humboldt	Light chocolate border to shadow on E wall.	Goodacre	B.A.A. Mem. 1898

No.	Date and Time	Feature or Location; Duration	Description	Observer	Reference
195	1598 Jan 8, 06ʰ30ᵐ	Tycho region	About mid-eclipse, shadow so dense that details of surface disappeared entirely, except that bright ray extending SSW from Tycho was clearly visible throughout its whole extent and continued so throughout eclipse. (Lunar eclipse.)	Chevremont	Chevremont 1898; Fisher 1924
196	1898 Apr 6-8	Schröter's Valley	Apparent volcanic activity.	W. H. Pickering	Pickering 1903
197	1898 Jul 3, 21ʰ17ᵐ	Proclus	Half hour after mid-eclipse, the crater shone with reddish light in shadow. (Lunar eclipse.)	Mayo	Mayo 1898; Fisher 1924
198	1900 Dec 27, 23ʰ58ᵐ	Aristarchus	During eclipse, Aristarchus brilliant. (Lunar eclipse.)	Stuyvaert	Nasmyth and Stuyvaert 1900-09; Fisher 1924
199	1901 Oct 23	Marius	A number of light streaks noticed on the crater floor. (Usually none are seen.)	Bolton	Bolton 1901
200	1902 Aug 13, 06ʰ36ᵐ	Near Lambert	(1) Brilliant starlike point; (2) completely round bright area, on dark side of moon's terminator, mag. 3 or 4.	Jones	(1) Pickering 1902; (2) Sirius 1903
201	1902 Oct 16	Theaetetus	Cloud near Theaetetus.	Charbonneaux	Charbonneaux 1902
202	1903 Mar 1	Aristarchus	Intermittent light "like a little star."	Rey	Rey 1903
203	1903 Mar 2	Aristarchus	Intermittent light "like a little star."	Glasury	Bull. Soc. Astr. France 1903
204	1903 Jul 31	Plato	Bright hazy object 2″ diameter on crater floor.	Pickering	Pickering 1906
205	1904 Oct 2, 13ʰ00ᵐ 16ʰ00ᵐ	Plato	Total or partial obscuration of crater floor.	Elger, Klein, Hodge, Goodacre	Goodacre 1931; Webb 1962 ed., Green 1965
206	1905 Feb 19, 19ʰ02ᵐ	Aristarchus	During eclipse, bright spot shining in the dark as a little star. (Lunar eclipse.)	Mayo	Mayo and Bussell 1905; Fisher 1924
207	1905 Aug 15, 03ʰ39ᵐ	Tycho	Visible, even brilliant during eclipse.	Rey	Sforza 1905; Fisher 1924

No.	Date and Time	Feature or Location; Duration	Description	Observer	Reference
208	1906 Aug 4, 12h 58m	Aristarchus	Shone conspicuously during lunar eclipse.	Ward	Ward 1906-07; Fisher 1924
209	1906	Mare Humorum		Flammarion	Arecado 1962
210	1906	Mare Serenitatis		Dubois, Flammarion	Arecado 1962
211	1906	Lichtenberg		Flammarion	Arecado 1962
212	1906	Alphonsus		Flammarion	Arecado 1962
213	1907 Jan 22	Plato	Glow of light in part of Plato.	Fauth	Fauth 1907
214	1909	Tycho	False dawn.	McHish	McHish 1909
215	1909	Mersenius	Dimly lighted zone W of shadow.	Merlin	Merlin 1909
216	1912 Apr 1, 22h 15m	Tycho	Visible-like a bright spot standing out in the dark slate-gray shadow. Only Tycho was seen during lunar eclipse.	LeRoy	LeRoy 1912; Fisher 1924
217	1912 May 19	Dark side	Small red glowing area noticed on shadow side of moon.	Valier	Valier 1912
218	1912 May 29	Leibnitz Mts. area	Glowing line of light into dark side.	Franks	Franks obs. book
219	1912 Sep 25	Pico B	Haze spreading from W end of crater.	Pickering	Eawstrea 1937
220	1913 Mar 22, 11h 15m		During eclipse totality, there remained visible to the NW only a luminous point not much larger than the planet Mars and of the same color. (Lunar eclipse.)	G. Jackson	Jackson 1913; Fisher 1924
221	1913 Jun 15	South	Distinct small reddish spot.	Maw	Webb 1962 ed.
222	1913 Jan 31	Littrow	Seven white spots arranged like a Greek gamma.	Burgess	Eng. Mech. Vol. 101
223	1915 Apr 21	S of Posidonius	Noted special occurrence S of large circle Posidonius which he took as evidence of water vapor.	Haselard	Haselard 1917
224	1915 Apr 23	Clavius	Narrow, straight beam of light from crater A to crater B.	Cook	B.A.A. Mem., 1936
225	1915 Dec 11	Mare Cristum	Particularly bright spot like star on N shore.	Thomas	Eng. Mech. Vol. 103

No.	Date and Time	Feature or Location, Duration	Description	Observer	Reference
226	1916 Oct 16	Plato	Pickering's craterlet No. 59 involved in reddish shadow and disappeared. Usually distinctly seen under similar illumination.	Maggini	Sci. Amer. 1939
227	1917 Jan 8, 6h 45m	Dionysius	Point on rim of crater shone like a small starlike sometimes after entering the eclipse shadow. (Lunar eclipse.)	W. F. A. Ellison	Ellison 1917; Fisher 1924
228	1919 Nov 7, 23h 45m	Tycho, vicinity	Long ray in direction of Longomontanus remained visible glowing in weak gray-green light during whole eclipse (until clouds stopped observation. (Lunar eclipse.)	Fock	Fock 1920; Fisher 1924
229	1920	Near Vitruvius	Some peaks varied considerably in brightness.	Franke	Wilkins and Moore 1955
230	1922 Nov 28	La Hire; 20 min	Shadow cut through by white streak.	H. P. Wilkins	Wilkins 1954
231	1927 May 12	Petvie A (Wilkins' Graham)	Complete obscuration of crater.	H. P. Wilkins	Moore 1953; Green 1965
232	1927 Dec 21, 22-00h	Petvie A (Wilkins' Graham)	Invisible.	H. P. Wilkins	H. P. Wilkins obs., book
233	1931 Feb 22	Aristarchus	Reddish-yellow.	Joslin	Joslin 1931
234	1931 Mar 27	Tycho	Central mountain gray, although crater interior was in full shadow.	Barker	Moore 1953; Green 1965
235	1931	Aristarchus	Bluish glare.	Goodacre, Molesworth	Goodacre 1931
236	1932 Apr 15, 08h 57m	Plato	Sudden appearance of white spot like cloud.	Goddard and Ivicol	Pop. Astr. 1932
237	1933 Mar 30	Aristarchus region	White.	Douillet	Douillet 1933
238	1933 Sep 1	Neighborhood of Pico, and Pico B	Haze observed.	Rawstron	Rawstron 1937
239	1933 Oct 1	Neighborhood of Pico, and Pico B	Haze observed.	Rawstron	Rawstron 1937
240	1936 May 4	Eratosthenes	Detected small bright spots on crater floor.	Martz	Haas 1942

No.	Date and Time	Feature or Location; Duration	Description	Observer	Reference
241	1936 Oct 4	Eratosthenes	Many small bright spots on crater floor, some of which Martz detected, but Johnson drew bright bands in their positions.	Haas	Haas 1942
242	1936 Oct 25	Eratosthenes	Small bright spots on floor of crater.	Haas	Haas 1942
243	1937 Feb 14	Cassini	Bright spot.	Andrenko	Azevedo 1962
244	1937 Sep 17	Aristarchus	Bright streak.	H. M. Johnson	Haas 1942
245	1937 Sep 29	Riccioli	Color of dark area was deep purple; and again same with vivid hue.	Haas	Haas 1942
246	1937 Oct 26	Alphonsus, Herschel, and Ptolemaeus	Milky floors.	Alter	Alter 1959
247	1937 Dec 12	Plato	Strongly marked streak of orange-brown on E wall.	Barker	Barker 1940
248	1938 Jan 16–17	Plato	Brownish gold-veined surface of color irregularly laid on smooth floor of crater.	Barker	Barker 1940
249	1938 Feb 1–	Plato	Golden-brown spot on E wall very prominent, with a yellowish glow without a definite boundary spreading over floor of crater.	Fox	Barker 1940
250	1939 Feb 23	Aristarchus	Bright spot.	Andrenko	Azevedo 1962
251	1939 Mar 29, 19"06"	Copernicus; 15 min	Central mountain group seen distinctly as diffuse light spot. Sunrise on peaks did not begin until 22"39".	Wilkins	Wilkins 1954
252	1939 Aug 4, 00"18"	Schickard	Dense fog.	Moore	Wilkins and Moore 1958; Firsoff 1962 ed., p. 80
253	1939 Oct 29	Macrobius	Floor of crater reddish-brown, a hue ordinarily absent.	Barcroft	Haas 1942
254	1939 Dec 27	Aristarchus	Slight bluish tinge on the still brilliant W wall.	Barcroft	Haas 1942; Firsoff 1962 ed., p. 84
255	1940 May 26, 23"40"	Schickard	Whitish obscuration; less dense than 1939 Aug 2.	Moore	Moore obs. book

No.	Date and Time	Feature or Location; Duration	Description	Observer	Reference
256	1940 Jun 14	Plato	Too hazy streaks of medium intensity, much obscures detail.	Haas	Haas 1942
257	1940 Jul 34	Tycho	Curious faint milky-looking luminosity seen. Luminous marks in shadow seem ragged-edged and irregularly shaped.	Haas	Haas 1942
258	1940 Oct 19	Lichtenberg area	Pronounced reddish-brown or orange color around area. Found color less marked next night, and slight by Oct 22.	Barcroft	Haas 1942; Strol. Astr. 1951
259	1940 Oct 29	Cusps	Prolongation of N horn by 15 degrees.	Vaughan	Firsoff 1962 ed., p. 127
260	1940 Dec ?	Aristarchus	Distinguished crater in dark hemisphere as a bright spot.	Vaughan	Haas 1942
261	1940 Dec 9	Tycho	Found some luminosity on W crater rim of W outer slope.	Barcroft	Haas 1942
262	1940 Dec 25	Cusps	"Each horn appeared prolonged by about 10 degrees."	Haas	Firsoff 1962 ed., p. 127
263	1941 Jan 6	Arzachel	Anomalous shadow.	Barcroft	Azevedo 1962; Wilkins 1954
264	1941 Feb 6	Conon	Faint bright spot, not too definite in outline, seen on crater floor.	Vaughan	Haas 1942
265	1941 Mar 6	Cusps	Prolongation suspected.	Barcroft	Firsoff 1962 ed., p. 127
266	1941 May 31	Aristarchus	Crater perceived by earthshine (Haas thought it must have been unusually brilliant).	Barcroft	Haas 1942
267	1941 Jul 10	Gassendi, and near Hansteen	Moving luminous speck near Hansteen, estimated diameter 0.1", mag >8 (lunar meteor?).	Haas	Wilkins and Moore 1958, p. 243; Azevedo 1962
268	1942 Feb 2, 18h26m–19h15m	W of Kepler; 55 min	Whitish glow near earthlit limb.	Y. W. L. Fisher	Wilkins and Moore 1958, p. 271
269	1942 Aug 26	Atlas	Dark areas faded in crater.	Haas	Haas 1965
270	1944 Apr 4	Hyginus N (Klein N)	Much darker than usual.	Wilkins	Moore 1953, p. 144; Green 1965

No.	Date and Time	Feature or Location; Duration	Description	Observer	Reference
271	1944 Aug 12, 23°00"	Plato	Exceptional darkness of crater floor; three light spots noted at foot of E wall. Although no light streaks were visible, there was a large and conspicuous spot near the center. Since this spot has been noted as slightly but definitely elongated all round, Wilkins suggested that temporary dark cloud or vapour may have covered true floor up to level of rim.	Wilkins	Wilkins 1944
272	1945 Aug 31	Schickard	Mist on crater floor.	Wilkins	Wilkins and Moore 1955
273	1945 Oct 19, 11°21'30"	Plato	Bright flash on crater floor near E wall.	Thornton	Green 1945; Thornton 1945
274	1945 Oct 19	Darwin	Three twilight points of light on wall.	Moore	Wilkins 1954
275	1947 Jan 30	Eratosthenes	Without normal shadow.	H. Hill	Wilkins and Moore 1955
276	1947 Aug 28	SE of Langrenus	Mountain on limb very decidedly bluish.	Rowe	Wilkins 1954
277	1947 Nov 30	Aristarchus	Bright spots on inner W slopes.	Firsoff	Wilkins 1954
278	1948 Feb 17	Dawes	Central peak not seen, but cleft-like marking from SW crest towards E shadow.	Thornton	Firsoff, fn Moore
279	1948 Apr 14	30 degrees N of Grimaldi on W limb	Prolongation of earthlight on cusp.	Wilkins	Wilkins 1954
280	1948 Apr 15		Bright spot on earthlit W limb 30 degrees N of Grimaldi and estimated equal to a 3rd mag star.	Vince	J.B.A.A. 1948
281	1948 May 29	NE of Phlolous, 15 min	Red glow.	Baum	Firsoff 1962 ed., p. 82
282	1948 Jul 2-22	Mare Crisium; several hours	Almost festoon-like apart from Picard, Peirce.	Moore	Moore obs. book
283	1948 Jul 27	Promontorium Heraclides	Blurred and misty.	Moore, Bochert	Moore obs. book
284	1948 Aug 3	Dark side	A small bright flash on earthlit portion . . . like a bright sparkle of frost on the ground.	Woodward	Moore 1953
285	1948 Aug 10	E of Picard; several hours	Two areas E of Picard appeared featureless.	Moore	J.B.A.A. 1949
286	1948 Oct ?	Barker's Quadrangle	Nebulous white patch in place of Quadrangle.	Moore	Moore obs. book

No.	Date and Time	Feature or Location, Duration	Description	Observer	References
287	1948 Oct 19	Proswodtlyan Heraclides	Blurred.	Docherty	Contrib. by Moore
288	1949 Feb 7, 18h00m	Kepler	White glow near Kepler.	V. W. t. Fisher	Contrib. by Moore
289	1949 Feb 9	Barker's Quadrangle	Quadrangle not seen... appeared misty.	Moore	Moore obs. book
290	1949 Feb 10	Schröter's Valley, near Cobrahead	Diffuse patch of thin smoke or vapor from W side of Schröter's Valley near Cobrahead, spreading into plain, detail indistinct, hazy (surrounding area clear).	Thornton	Wilkins and Moore 1955, p. 289
291	1949 May 3, 20h00m	Barker's Quadrangle	Whole area hazy.	Moore	Moore obs. book
292	1949 May 1	Aristarchus	Visible in earthshine, glowing suddenly as diffuse light patch.	Wilkins	Wilkins 1954
293	1949 Oct 7, 02h54m	Aristarchus	Abnormally bright during lunar eclipse.	G. Broon, Haye	Contrib. by Moore
294	1949 Nov 3, 01h06m	Aristarchus	Blue glare, base inner W wall.	Bartlett	Bartlett 1967
295	1950 Jun 27, 02h30m	Aristarchus	Blue glare, base inner W wall.	Bartlett	Bartlett 1967
296	1950 Jun 27	Herodotus	Bright point in crater.	Bartlett	Strol. Astr. 1962
297	1950 Jun 28, 03h27m	Aristarchus	Blue glare, rim of W wall.	Bartlett	Bartlett 1967
298	1950 Jun 29, 05h30m	Aristarchus	Strong bluish glare, E, SE wall.	Bartlett	Bartlett 1967
299	1950 Jul 28, 02h52m	Aristarchus	Blue glare, base inner W wall.	Bartlett	Bartlett 1967
300	1950 Jul 31, 04h30m	Aristarchus	Violet glare, E, NE rim.	Bartlett	Bartlett 1967
301	1950 Aug 28, 04h25m	Aristarchus	Intense blue-violet glare; E wall bright spot, E, NE rim.	Bartlett	Bartlett 1967
302	1951 Jan 21	E of Lichtenberg	Red patch.	Baum	Strol. Astr. 1951

No.	Date and Time	Feature or Location; Duration	Description	Observer	Reference
303	1951 Feb 4, 21ʰ 08ᵐ – 23ʰ 08ᵐ	W of Endymion; 2 hr	Mist over peak.	Baum	Baum 1966
304	1951 May 17	Gassendi	Bright speck of short duration.	Wilkins	Moore 1953, p. 118
305	1951 Aug 20	W. H. Pickering (Messier A)	Brilliant white patch inside crater.	Moore	Moore 1953, p. 147
306	1951 Oct 20	W. H. Pickering (Messier A)	Bright circular patch.	Moore	Moore obs. book
307	1952 Apr 3		Twenty-one spots were charted, one surrounded by a light area, while three streaks were seen in the NW quarter.	Wilkins, Moore	Wilkins and Moore 1955
308	1952 Apr 4	Plato	Obscuration of crater floor.	Cragg	Moore 1953, 1965
309	1952 Sep 9, 23ʰ 00ᵐ	Calippus	Broad hazy band of light across floor (observer gave observation low weight).	Moore	Moore obs. book
310	1952 Dec 24	Theaetetus	Hazy line of light.	Moore	Wilkins and Moore 1958, p. 238
311	1953 Apr 18		Faint extension of cusps.	Wilkins	Wilkins 1953
312	1953 Nov 15, 02ʰ 00ᵐ	Near Pallas	Very bright spot on illuminated part near terminator seen and photographed.	Suart	Strolling Astr. 1956; Suart 1957
313	1954 Mar 21	Atlas	Violet tint in Atlas.	Delmotte	Delmotte
314	1954 May 10	Crater in Ptolemaeus	Flash.	Firsoff	Firsoff 1962 ed., p. 53
315	1954 May 11, 20ʰ 30ᵐ	Eratosthenes	Central mountain group invisible, though surrounding details were clear.	Cattermole	Cattrib. by Moore
316	1954 Jul 14, 04ʰ 30ᵐ	Aristarchus	E wall bright spot; violet glare.	Bartlett	Bartlett 1967
317	1954 Jul 16, 03ʰ 32ᵐ	Aristarchus	Whole interior of strong violet tint; violet tint in nimbus and N and NE of crater.	Bartlett	Bartlett 1967
318	1954 Jul 17, 02ʰ 00ᵐ	Aristarchus	Pale violet tint on surface NE of crater; no color elsewhere.	Bartlett	Bartlett 1967
319	1954 Jul 24, 02ʰ 19ᵐ	Aristarchus	Crater filled with pale violet light.	Bartlett	Bartlett 1967

No.	Date and Time	Feature or Location; Duration	Description	Observer	Reference
320	1954 Aug 13, 22ʰ 00ᵐ	Aristarchus	Brilliant in red (filter), variable.	Firsoff	Firsoff 1962
321	1954 Aug 18	Aristarchus	Brilliant blue-violet glare over E and NE walls.	Bartlett	Contrib. by Moore
322	1954 Sep 8, 20ʰ00ᵐ	Proclus	Brightness variation in blue light.	Firsoff	Firsoff 1962 et, p. 83
323	1954 Oct 8,10	Timocharis	Red glow.	Firsoff	Firsoff 1962, 1966
324	1954 Oct 11, 04ʰ57ᵐ	Aristarchus	Violet tint on floor, E wall and central peak; pale emitted.	Bartlett	Bartlett 1967
325	1954 Oct 12, 03ʰ32ᵐ	Aristarchus	Pale violet radiance, S wall, SE, E, SE walls, central peak.	Bartlett	Bartlett 1967
326	1954 Oct 12, 04ʰ03ᵐ	Aristarchus	Strong violet tint E half of floor; very faint W half of floor and W wall. Dark violet in nimbus; pale violet on plateau.	Bartlett	Bartlett 1967
327	1954 Oct 13, 02ʰ06ᵐ	Aristarchus	Bright blue-violet glare, E rim; pale violet radiance within crater and around S wall bright spot. Dark violet in nimbus; pale violet on plateau.	Bartlett	Bartlett 1967
328	1954 Oct 13, 03ʰ15ᵐ	Aristarchus	Scarcely perceivable violet radiance within crater; wall bands look faint.	Bartlett	Bartlett 1967
329	1954 Oct 18, 06ʰ47ᵐ	Aristarchus	Strong blue-violet glare, E wall bright spot, E wall and on central peak.	Bartlett	Bartlett 1967
330	1954 Nov 5	Copernicus	Bright point.	Johnstone	Strol. Astr. 1962
331	1954 Nov 7, 23ʰ20ᵐ	Kepler	Bright point just outside E wall.	Lage	J.B.A.A. 1965
332	1954 Nov 12, 02ʰ42ᵐ	Aristarchus	Blue-violet glare; E wall bright spot and whole length of E wall. Suspected violet tint in N and NE of crater; certain on plateau. Greatly faded by 05ʰ05ᵐ.	Bartlett	Bartlett 1967

No.	Date and Time	Feature or Location; Duration	Description	Observer	Reference
333	1954 Dec 12, 02ʰ44ᵐ	Aristarchus	Strong violet glare, E rim, changing to brown.	Bartlett	Bartlett 1967
334	1955 Jan 8, 00ʰ46ᵐ	Aristarchus	Strong violet glare whole length of E rim, brightest SE and around E wall bright spot.	Bartlett	Bartlett 1967
335	1955 Jan 12, 04ʰ54ᵐ	Aristarchus	Blue-violet glare; E wall bright spot, E, NE rim.	Bartlett	Bartlett 1967
336	1955 Apr 2, 02ʰ28ᵐ – 03ʰ08ᵐ	Straight-wall region; ~1 hr 40 min	Small craters between Birt and fault invisible; at times under excellent seeing conditions, while craterlets on E side were continually observed.	Capen	Capen 1955, 1967
337	1955 Apr 5, 03ʰ25ᵐ	Aristarchus	E wall and glacis: violet; uncertain.	Bartlett	Bartlett 1967
338	1955 Apr 24	Near Possidonius	White flash of short duration N of Mare Serenitatis near Possidonius.	Wykes	Strol. Astr. 1955
339	1956 May 5, 03ʰ33ᵐ	Aristarchus	Pale violet tint in E half of floor; violet band at base, E side of central peak.	Bartlett	Bartlett 1967
340	1955 May 2–8	Lichtenberg	"Glitter" suggesting electrical discharge.	Nicolini	Aeronin 1962
341	1955 May 24	Near South Pole		Firsoff	Firsoff 1962 ed., p. 131
342	1955 Jun 25, 20ʰ30ᵐ	Theophilus	Mistiness; absent the next night.	Firsoff	Firsoff 1962 ed., p. 84
343	1955 Jul 3, 22ʰ00ᵐ	Schröter's Valley	Starlike point.	Firsoff	Firsoff 1962 ed., Pl. X
344	1955 Jul 13	Aristarchus	Brilliant in blue and green.	Firsoff	Firsoff 1966
345	1955 Aug 1, 04ʰ30ᵐ	Aristarchus	Plateau only: pale violet tint.	Bartlett	Bartlett 1967
346	1955 Aug 3	Manilius, Timocharis	Manilius extraordinarily brilliant; Timocharis bright in blue, appears large and diffuse.	Firsoff	Firsoff 1966

No.	Date and Time	Feature or Location; Duration	Description	Observer	Reference
347	1955 Aug 28	Near Carpathians; ~25 sec	Bright flare on dark side similar to 2nd mag star.	McTavish	Sky and Tel., 1955
348	1955 Aug 30; 65°-40°	Aristarchus	Floor, base inner W wall, NW wall: faint bluish glare.	Bartlett	Bartlett 1967
349	1955 Sep 7; 63°-26°	Copernicus	Brightened in blue.	Firsoff	Firsoff 1959
350	1955 Sep 7; 64°-52°	Aristarchus	Strong blue-violet glare; E, NE rim; also E base of central peak. Dark violet, nimbus.	Bartlett	Bartlett 1967
351	1955 Sep 8; 64°-52°	Aristarchus	Strong bluish glare on E, NE wall, on E edge of E wall bright spot, and bordering both edges of the bright floor band, passing around W of central peak. Dark violet tint in nimbus.	Bartlett	Bartlett 1967
352	1955 Sep 8	Taurus Mountains	Two flashes from edge of Taurus Mountains.	Lambert	Sky and Tel., 1955
353	1955 Sep 9; 62°-54°	Aristarchus	Floor: blue clay color.	Bartlett	Bartlett 1967
354	1955 Sep 28; 35°-00°	Calabrabat	Obscured by brown patch.	Bostwick	Cond'tls, by Moore
355	1955 Oct 2; 65°-42°	Aristarchus	Violet glare, E, NE rim. Over E wall bright spot resembled a violet mist. Center itself was hazy; could not get sharp focus.	Bartlett	Bartlett 1967
356	1955 Oct 4; 44°-55°	Aristarchus	Pale violet tint; E wall bright spot and whole length of E rim; dark violet in nimbus.	Bartlett	Bartlett 1967
357	1955 Oct 4°	Aristarchus	Spectrum enhanced in B and K region.	Kozyrev	Kozyrev 1957
358	1955 Oct 5; 65°-44°	Aristarchus	Intensely bright blue-violet glare; E wall bright spot, E, NE wall.	Bartlett	Bartlett 1967
359	1955 Oct 31; 66°-40°	Aristarchus	Bright blue-violet glare, E, NE rim; dark violet hue in nimbus; pale violet radiance over plateau.	Bartlett	Bartlett 1967

No.	Date and Time	Feature or Location; Duration	Description	Observer	Reference
360	1955 Oct 31, 04:50"	Aristarchus	Intense blue-violet glare, E, NE rim. Dark violet in nimbus; pale violet on plateau.	Bartlett	Bartlett 1967
361	1955 Oct 31, 19:00"	Cobrahead	Dark blue obscuration.	Milligan	Comrh. by Moore
362	1955 Nov 1, 02:18"	Aristarchus	Pale violet tint, E wall bright spot, E, NE rim, dark violet hue in nimbus.	Bartlett	Bartlett 1967
363	1955 Nov 6, 05:50"	Aristarchus	Strong blue-violet glare, E, NE wall. Dark violet hue in nimbus.	Bartlett	Bartlett 1967
364	1955 Nov 27, 02:43"	Aristarchus	Floor; blue clay color.	Bartlett	Bartlett 1967
365	1955	Plato		Sytinskaya	Azvoado 1962
366	1955	Aristarchus		Sytinskaya	Azvoado 1962
367	1955	Tycho		Sytinskaya	Azvoado 1962
368	1956 Jan 23	W edge of Cavendish ~50 min	Variable point of light.	Houghton, Warner	Strol. Astr. 1955
369	1956 Jan 27, 01:18"	Aristarchus	Violet glare whole length of E wall and around E wall bright spot; violet tint N and NE of crater.	Bartlett	Bartlett 1967
370	1956 Jan 28, 02:32"	Aristarchus	Pale violet radiance; E, NE rim.	Bartlett	Bartlett 1967
371	1956 Mar 14, 19:00"		Twilight at 8 cusp traced 400 mi. beyond cusp. No trace of twilight at N pole, 4½ inch reflector used. Moon 2½ days old.	Firsoff	J.B.A.A. 1956
372	1956 Mar 18		Anomalous dimming of α Tau and 195 Tau before occultation.	Firsoff	J.B.A.A. 1956
373	1956 Jan 29, 02:39"	Aristarchus	Blue glare, base inner W wall.	Bartlett	Bartlett 1967
374	1956 Jan 29, 02:42"	Aristarchus	Intense blue-violet glare, on E wall bright spot. Dark violet in nimbus.	Bartlett	Bartlett 1967
375	1956 Jan 18, 06:55"	Aristarchus	Intense blue-violet glare, E wall bright spot. Dark violet, nimbus. Pale violet N and SE of crater and on plateau.	Bartlett	Bartlett 1967
376	1956 Jan 29, 06:30"	Aristarchus	Faint, blue-violet tint; E wall bright spot.	Bartlett	Bartlett 1967

No.	Date and Time	Feature or Location Duration	Description	Observer	Reference
377	1956 Jun 30, 06h55m	Aristarchus	Violet blue-violet glare; E wall bright spot, E, NE wall.	Bartlett	Bartlett 1967
378	1956 Jul 28, 05h46m	Aristarchus	Vivid blue-violet glare on central peak, band across E floor to E wall bright spot, on E wall bright spot, and E, NE wall. Absent by 07h28m.	Bartlett	Bartlett 1967
379	1956 Oct 16, 05h34m	Aristarchus	Blue glare, base inner W wall.	Bartlett	Bartlett 1967
380	1956 Oct 20, 06h15m	Aristarchus	Bright blue-violet glare on E wall bright spot, E, NE rim. Dark violet in nimbus.	Bartlett	Bartlett 1967
381	1956 Oct 26	Alphonsus	A suspected partial obscuration of the floor based on disagreemes in detail in infrared and ultra-violet photographs.	Alter	Alter 1956, 1959
382	1956 Nov 15, 01h17m	Aristarchus	Faint blue radiance, base inner W wall.	Bartlett	Bartlett 1967
383	1956 Nov 16, 00h25m	Aristarchus	Floor: bright bluish tint F of central peak; blue-gray W of central peak.	Bartlett	Bartlett 1967
384	1956 Nov 17-28	Aristarchus, Tycho, Kepler, Proclus, Menilius, Byrgius	Extraordinarily bright.	Argenbrite, et al.	Acevedo 1962
385	1956	Tycho		Dubois	Acevedo 1962
386	1956	Mare Humorum		Vigroux	Acevedo 1962
387	1957 Mar 17, 06h24m	Aristarchus	Strong violet glare; E wall bright spot and whole length of E wall. Dark violet in nimbus; pale violet on plateau.	Bartlett	Bartlett 1967
388	1957 Mar 18, 06h43m	Aristarchus	Strong violet glare; E wall bright spot, E wall. Very strong violet hue in nimbus.	Bartlett	Bartlett 1967
389	1957 Jun 11, 04h45m	Aristarchus	Floor: uniform bluish radiance.	Bartlett	Bartlett 1967

No.	Date and Time	Feature or Location; Duration	Description	Observer	Reference
390	1957 Jul 11, 05°49°	Aristarchus	Pale violet radiance in crater and on plateau.	Bartlett	Bartlett 1967
391	1957 Aug 18, 06°58°	Aristarchus	Pale blue tint on all walls; floor dazzling white.	Bartlett	Bartlett 1967
392	1957 Oct 11, 05°15°	Aristarchus	Bright blue-violet; E wall bright spot, E, NE rim. Dark violet in nimbus.	Bartlett	Bartlett 1967
393	1957 Oct 2, 02°40°	Aristarchus	Bright blue-violet glare; E wall bright spot, E, NE, N, NW walls. Dark violet, nimbus.	Bartlett	Bartlett 1967
394	1957 Oct 12	Aristarchus; 1 hr	Bright flash; then brownish concentric patch.	Bachillo and daughter	Cameron 1965
395	1957 Oct 13, 03°00°	Aristarchus	Weak violet glare; whole length of E wall.	Bartlett	Bartlett 1967
396	1957 Oct 13	In or near Aristarchus	Bright spot of light ("explosion").	Haas	Haas 1957
397	1957 Oct 15, 05°45°	Aristarchus	Strong blue-violet glare, whole length of E wall.	Bartlett	Bartlett 1967
398	1957 Oct 16, 06°00°	Aristarchus	Faint blue-gray tint. N, NW, W floor and walls.	Bartlett	Bartlett 1967
399	1958 May 1, 03°40°	Aristarchus	Entire sunlit area of floor, bluish.	Bartlett	Bartlett 1967
400	1958 May 4, 05°28°	Aristarchus	Blue-violet glare S side of E wall bright spot; dark violet to nimbus; pale violet on plateau.	Bartlett	Bartlett 1967
401	1958 May 31, 03°40°	Aristarchus	Pale blue-gray floor; violet band E base of central peak.	Bartlett	Bartlett 1967
402	1958 Jun 29, 04°04°	Aristarchus	Floor: very pale bluish tint.	Bartlett	Bartlett 1967
403	1958 Jul 2, 06°22°	Aristarchus	Strong violet glare whole length of E wall, involving E wall bright spot; dark violet, nimbus.	Bartlett	Bartlett 1967

No.	Date and Time	Feature or Location	Duration	Description	Observer	Reference
404	1958 Jul 3, 07ʰ06ᵐ	Aristarchus		Bright blue-violet glare: E, NE rim. Dark violet, nimbus: pale violet, plateau.	Bartlett	Bartlett 1967
405	1958 Aug 2, 06ʰ15ᵐ	Aristarchus		Strong violet glare; E wall bright spot, NE wall. Dark violet, nimbus. Strong violet, plateau.	Bartlett	Bartlett 1967
406	1958 Sep 1, 07ʰ22ᵐ	Aristarchus		Whole crater filled with pale violet radiancy, especially bright on walls. Pale violet N and NE of crater and on plateau.	Bartlett	Bartlett 1967
407	1958 Sep 23	Pitao		Became enveloped in an obscuring cloud-like mist.	Moore	Moore obs. book
408	1958 Oct 26	N of Mare Crisium		Bright spot in dark area of moon.	Mayenson	Mayenson 1965
409	1958 Nov 3, 02ʰ00ᵐ	Alphonsus		Reddish glow, followed by effusion of gas.	Kozyrev	Kozyrev 1959, 1963; Green 1965
410	1958 Nov 19, 04ʰ00ᵐ – 04ʰ30ᵐ	Alphonsus	30 min	Diffuse cloud over central mountain.	Poppendeik, Band	Alter 1959; Poppendeik and Band 1959
411	1958 Nov 19, 22ʰ05ᵐ	Alpetragius		Portion of shadow in crater vanished.	Stein	Stein 1959
412	1958 Nov 19	Alphonsus		Reddish patch close to central peak.	Wilkins, Hole	Wilkins 1959; Hole 1959
413	1958 Nov 22	Alphonsus		Grey spot.	Barthz	Moore 1965
414	1958 Dec 19	Alphonsus		Reddish patch close to central peak.	Wilkins, Hole	Wilkins 1959; Hole 1959; Moore 1965
415	1959 Jan 22	Aristarchus		Interior, light brilliant blue, later turning white.	Alter	Alter NASA Report
416	1959 Jan 23	Aristarchus		Brilliant blue interior.	Alter	Cameron 1965
417	1959 Feb 18	Alphonsus		Red patch.	Hole	Moore 1965
418	1959 Mar 24, 02ʰ33ᵐ and 04ʰ55ᵐ	Aristarchus		Strong blue and blue-violet glares, E wall, E wall bright spot, S wall bright spot, intermittent display. Observation at 04ʰ55ᵐ of same phenomena.	Bartlett	Bartlett 1967

No.	Date and Time	Feature or Location; Duration	Description	Observer	Reference
419	1959 Mar 25, 03h 24m	Aristarchus	Intense blue-violet glare on whole length of E rim and on E wall bright spot; dark violet hue in nimbus.	Bartlett	Bartlett 1967
420	1959 Apr 19	W of Mare Humorum	Bright point to W of mare.	McFarlane	Strol. Astr. 1959
421	1959 Sep 5	Aristarchus	Irregular, intermittent starlike point of light, 8th to 9th mag, appeared within bright area. No color seen.	Rule	Rule 1959
422	1959 Sep 13	Littrow	Obliterated by a hovering cloud (Feist disagrees with Bradford).	Bradford	Cootrth, by Moore
423	1959 Oct 23h	Alphonsus	Red glow seen. Spectrum showed unusual features.	Kozyrev	Kozyrev 1962
424	1960 Jan 6	Alphonsus	Red spot.	Warner	J. Int. Lunar Soc. 1960
425	1960 Nov	Piton: ~30 min	Red obscuration concealing peak.	Schaeller	Cameron 1965
426	1960 Dec	Piton	Red obscuration less intense than in November.	Schaeller	Cameron 1965
427	1961 Jan	Piton	Red obscuration less intense than in November.	Schaeller	Cameron 1965
428	1961 Feb 15h, ~08h 41m	Aristarchus, Plato	Seen as bright features during solar eclipse (on film of eclipse shown by BBC May 6, 1966).	Sartory, Middlehurst	Cootrth, by Middlehurst
429	1961 May 30–31h	Aristarchus	Enhancement of spectrum in UV.	Grainger, Ring	Grainger and Ring 1963
430	1961 Jun 27–28h	Aristarchus, ray near Bessel	Enhancement of spectrum in UV.	Grainger, Ring	Grainger and Ring 1963
431	1961 Jun 29–30h	E of Plato	Enhancement of spectrum in UV.	Grainger, Ring	Grainger and Ring 1963
432	1961 Oct 19	Eratosthenes	Bright spot in crater.	Bartlett	Strol. Astr. 1962
433	1961 Nov 26h	Aristarchus region	Red glow seen. Anomalous spectra in red and blue.	Kozyrev	Kozyrev 1963
434	1961 Nov 28h	Aristarchus region	Red glow seen. Anomalous spectra in red and blue.	Kozyrev	Kozyrev 1963
435	1961 Dec 3h	Aristarchus region	Red glow seen. Anomalous spectra in red and blue.	Kozyrev	Kozyrev 1963

No.	Date and Time	Feature or Location; Duration	Description	Observer	Reference
436	1962 Sep 5	Region of Walter near terminator; 7 min	Faint point of light.	Cork	Cameron 1965
437	1962 Sep 16	"Whole moon"	Spectrum showed UV emission, particularly in region of H and K lines by comparison with spectra of Sun, Mars, and Jupiter.	Spinrad	Spinrad 1964
438	1962 Oct 8	Aristarchus; 1 hr	Activity.	Adams	Cameron 1965
439	1962 Oct 51	Aristarchus region	Enhancement of 30 percent at 3550 Å.	Searle	Searle 1965
440	1962 Oct 29	Aristarchus region	Color changes: reddish-orange to ruby patches.	Greenacre, Barr	Greenacre 1963
441	1963 Oct 30	Cobrahead; 7 min	Brightened area, 7th to 11th mag.	Bodien, Farrell	Cameron 1965
442	1963 Nov 1ʰ, 23ʰ00ᵐ	Near Kepler; 20 min	Enhancement of large area in red light.	Kopal, Rackham	Kopal and Rackham 1964a, 1964b; Shorthill 1965; Green 1965, p. 409
443	1963 Nov 11	Aristarchus	Color changes.	Jacobs	Greenacre 1963
444	1963 Sep 28	Aristarchus, Schroter's Valley; 1 hr 15 min	Red spots, then violet, blue haze.	Greenacre, et al.	Cameron 1965
445	1963 Nov 28	Cobrahead; 25 min	Pink spot on W side.	Tombaugh	Cameron 1965
446	1963 Nov 28	Aristarchus, Anaximander; 1 hr	Red spot in Aristarchus ow) and also on N edge of Anaximander.	W. Fisher	Cameron 1965
447	1963 Dec 28, 15ʰ55ᵐ - 16ʰ26ᵐ	Aristarchus-Herodotus; 31 min	Extensive red area.	9 students at Hiroshima, Japan	Sato 1964
448	1963 Dec 29–30, 23ʰ06ᵐ - 03ʰ08ᵐ	Aristarchus region; 5 hr	Purplish-blue patch.	Doherty and others	Contrib. by Moore
449	1963 Dec 30ᵈ, 11ʰ00ᵐ	NE limb; 20 min	During eclipse, anomalous reddish glow inside umbra. (Lunar eclipse.)	Many observers	Sky and Tel. 1964
450	1964 Feb 25	Cobrahead; 3 min, Aristarchus; 1 min	Red flashes, ~ 12 mag.	Bodine	Cameron 1965

No.	Date and Time	Feature or Location; Duration	Description	Observer	Reference
451	1964 Mar 14	Aristarchus	Sudden red glow on SW rim.	Leonna	Cameron 1965
452	1964 Mar 18	Aristarchus	Flash.	Earl and brother	Cameron 1965
453	1964 Mar 25, 06^{h}37^m	Aristarchus	Float; blue clay color.	Bartlett	Bartlett 1967
454	1964 Mar 25, 07^{h}59^m	Aristarchus	Blue-violet glare, E wall and N wall; E wall bright spot; violet tinge in nimbus.	Bartlett	Bartlett 1967
455	1964 Apr 22	Near Ross D	Bright spot.	Cross and others	Harris 1967
456	1964 Apr 26	Region of Censorinus	Surface brightening somewhat similar to Kopal-Rackham (1963 Nov 1) event.	Hopmann	Hopmann 1966
457	1964 May 17	Theophilus	Crimson color on W rim, 30 msg.	Dicke	Cameron 1965
458	1964 May 18, 02^{h}55^m–05^{h}00^m	SE of Ross D, 1 hr, 5 min	White obscuration moved 20 mph, decreased in extent. Photometron repeated, Newtonians 8" f/7 and 9" f/7 used.	Harris, Cross and others	Cameron 1965; Harris 1967
459	1964 May 20	Plato; 10 min	Strong orange-red color on W rim of crater, >10 mag.	Bartlett	Greenacre 1965
460	1964 May 26, 04^{h}22^m	Aristarchus	Strong blue-violet glare, E wall and E wall bright spot, strong violet tinge in nimbus.	Bartlett	Bartlett 1967
461	1964 May 28, 05^{h}38^m	Aristarchus	Blue-violet glare; E, NE wall. Dark violet hue in nimbus.	Bartlett	Bartlett 1967
462	1964 May 30, 07^{h}21^m	Aristarchus	Bright blue-violet glare; E wall bright spot, E, NE walls. Dark violet, nimbus.	Bartlett	Bartlett 1967
463	1964 Jun 6	Aristarchus area; 30 min	Spur between Aristarchus and Herodotus; red spots (dots) in Schröter's Valley.	Schmilling, St. Clair, Platt	Cameron 1965
464	1964 Jun 17	SE of Ross D	Moving bright spot, 2 brief obscurations of part of wall. Newtonian, 19" f/7.	Cross, Harris	Harris 1967
465	1964 Jun 20, 05^{h}00^m	Aristarchus	Nimbus only dark violet hue.	Bartlett	Bartlett 1967
466	1964 Jun 21, 02^{h}15^m–05^{h}14^m	S of Ross D, 2 hr, 1 min	Moving dark area, Newtonian 19" f/7.	Harris, Cross, Helland	Harris 1967

No.	Date and Time	Feature or Location; Duration	Description	Observer	References
467	1964 Jun 22, 04h55m	Aristarchus	Blue-violet glare, NE rim, streak; violet tinge in nimbus.	Bartlett	Bartlett 1967
468	1964 Jun 24, 01h05m	Aristarchus	Very bright during eclipse (direct photograph, lunar eclipse).	Fisher	Bernad on Dasguloring 1967
469	1964 Jun 25, 01h05m	Grimaldi	During lunar eclipse, white streak from Grimaldi toward limb.	Acosta	Lefort to Moore
470	1964 Jun 26, 05h24m	Aristarchus	Dark violet in nimbus; pale violet on plateau. Mascon (from earlier).	Bartlett	Bartlett 1967
471	1964 Jun 27, 05h43m	Aristarchus	Bright blue-violet, E wall bright spot, E, NE rim. Dark violet in nimbus.	Bartlett	Bartlett 1967
472	1964 Jun 28, 06h44m	Aristarchus	Blue-violet glare; E wall bright spot, E, NE, N, NW walls.	Bartlett	Bartlett 1967
473	1964 Jun 28	S region of Aristarchus	Reddish-brown tone observed.	Bartlett	Greenacre 1965
474	1964 Jul 16	SE of Ross D	Temporary "hill," est 3 km diam and shadow seen.	Cragg	Harris 1967
475	1964 Jul 17	Plato	Extra giant bands at base of inner W wall and on rim of N wall.	Bartlett	Greenacre 1965
476	1964 Jul 18	SE of Ross D	Bright area moved and shrank. Extent greater with amber filter.	Harris	Harris 1967
477	1964 Jul 18	Plato, some minutes	Pink tinge to W wall, 10th mag.	Bartlett	Cameron 1965
478	1964 Jul 28, 04h43m	Aristarchus	Blue-violet glare, E wall bright spot. Dark violet in nimbus; pale violet on plateau.	Bartlett	Bartlett 1967
479	1964 Jul 29, 03h50m	Aristarchus	Nimbus only; dark violet hue.	Bartlett	Bartlett 1967
480	1964 Jul 31, 05h28m	Aristarchus	Pale blue tint. NE, N, NW walls and floor.	Bartlett	Bartlett 1967
481	1964 Aug 16, 04h18m–05h29m	SE of Ross D, 1 hr, 2 min	Bright area. Confirmations varying with time.	Harris, Cross	Harris 1967
482	1964 Aug 24, 04h22m	Aristarchus	Bright blue-violet; E wall bright spot, E, NE wall.	Bartlett	Bartlett 1967
483	1964 Aug 25, 04h58m	Aristarchus	Bright blue-violet, E wall bright spot, E, NE rim. Dark violet in nimbus.	Bartlett	Bartlett 1967

No.	Date and Time	Feature or Location; Duration	Description	Observer	Reference
484	1964 Aug 26, 04°16"	Aristarchus	Blue–violet glare; E wall bright spot, E, NE rim. Dark violet hue in nimbus.	Bartlett	Bartlett 1967
485	1964 Aug 26	Aristarchus; ~1 hr	Red and blue bands.	Geniet, Bold	Cameron 1965
486	1964 Aug 27, 04°37"	Aristarchus	Blue–violet glare; E wall bright spot, E, NE wall. Dark violet, nimbus; pale violet on plateau.	Bartlett	Bartlett 1967
487	1964 Aug 28, 04°40"	Aristarchus	Faint blue–violet radiance, E wall bright spot and NE rim. Dark violet in nimbus.	Bartlett	Bartlett 1967
488	1964 Sep 15, 01°15"	Aristarchus	Craterlet, base NW wall; bluish.	Bartlett	Bartlett 1967
489	1964 Sep 28	Aristarchus–Herodotus	Several red spots in area.	Crosse, Cross	Cameron 1965
490	1964 Sep 29	SE of Bessel D	Bright obscuration.	Cross	Cameron 1965 / Harris 1967
491	1964 Sep 22, 03°05"	Aristarchus	Bright blue–violet glare; E wall bright spot and NE rim. Dark violet in nimbus.	Bartlett	Bartlett 1967
492	1964 Sep 22	Kunowsky; ~1 hr	Red area blinked in blinker.	Gibeauey, Hall, L. Johnson	Cameron 1965
493	1964 Sep 23, 03°30"	Aristarchus	Blue–violet flare (glare?); E wall bright spot, E, NE, N, NW wall.	Bartlett	Bartlett 1967
494	1964 Sep 25, 04°05"	Aristarchus	Blue–violet glare; E wall bright spot. Dark violet on nimbus.	Bartlett	Bartlett 1967
495	1964 Sep 25, 04°15"	Aristarchus	Blue–violet glare; E wall bright spot. Dark violet in nimbus; pale violet on plateau.	Bartlett	Bartlett 1967
496	1964 Sep 26, 05°07"	Aristarchus	Moderately intense; E wall bright spot. Dark violet, nimbus.	Bartlett	Bartlett 1967
497	1964 Oct 22, 02°09"	Aristarchus	Strong blue tint E half of floor; blue–violet glare, base E side central peak.	Bartlett	Bartlett 1967

No.	Date and Time	Feature or Location Describes	Description	Observer	Reference
498	1964 Oct 22, 02h12m	Aristarchus	Blue-violet glare, E wall bright spot, E, NE wall. Dark violet hue in nimbus.	Bartlett	Bartlett 1967
499	1964 Oct 24, 04h02m	Aristarchus	Blue-violet glares E wall bright spot, E, NE rim. Dark violet hue in nimbus.	Bartlett	Bartlett 1967
500	1964 Oct 25, 04h15m	Aristarchus	Nimbus only, dark violet hue.	Bartlett	Bartlett 1967
501	1964 Oct 25, 04h37m	Aristarchus	Blue-violet glare, E wall bright spot, E, NE wall. Faint violet tinge in nimbus.	Bartlett	Bartlett 1967
502	1964 Oct 26, 04h22m	Aristarchus	Nimbus only, dark violet hue.	Bartlett	Bartlett 1967
503	1964 Oct 27	Alphonsus	Reddish-pink patch at base of sunlit central peak.	L. Johnson, et al.	Cameron 1965
504	1964 Nov 14	Plato	Peak on W wall very brilliant white. At foot of peak on inner side, strong blue band. Immediately adjacent, on SE was a small, bright, red spot.	Bartlett	Greenacre 1965
505	1964 Nov 21, 04h57m	Aristarchus	Bright blue-violet glare. SE, N, and NW rims.	Bartlett	Bartlett 1967
506	1964 Nov 23, 03h29m	Aristarchus	Strong blue-violet glare: N, NE, NW walls. Dark violet, nimbus.	Bartlett	Bartlett 1967
507	1964 Nov 24, 04h50m	Aristarchus	Blue-violet glare, N rim. Dark violet in nimbus, pale violet N and NE of crater.	Bartlett	Bartlett 1967
508	1964 Dec 19	Aristarchus; 2 min	Brightened by a factor of 5.	Bodine, Farrell	Cameron 1965
509	1964 Dec 19, 02h45m		Anomalous bright area during lunar eclipse.	S. Hill and student	Hill 1966
510	1964 Dec 19, 02h35m	Edge of Mare Noctium	Photoelectric photometry showed strong anomalous enhancement of radiation during lunar eclipse.	Sandaleak, Stock	Sandaleak and Stock 1965

No.	Date and Time	Feature or Location; Duration	Description	Observer	Reference
511	1965 Mar 14, 05h 10m	SE of Ross D	Crater wall partially obscured. Bright area. Cassegrain 12", f/15.	Cross	Harris 1967
512	1965 Jul 1	Aristarchus, dark side	Starlike image.	Emanuel	Cameron 1965
513	1965 Jul 2	Aristarchus; 1 hr 21 min	Bright spot like star on dark side, estimated mag 4.	Emanuel, et al.	Greenacre 1965
514	1965 Jul 3	Aristarchus; ~1 hr 10 min	Pulsating spot on dark side.	Emanuel, et al.	Greenacre 1965
515	1965 Jul 4	Aristarchus; 1 hr	Bright spot, no pulsations, on dark side.	Emanuel, et al.	Greenacre 1965
516	1965 Jul 7	Grimaldi	White streak extended toward limb.	Arecato, et al.	Revista Astr. 1965
517	1965 Jul 9	Theophilus; 10 min	Bright spot.	Cross	Cameron 1965; Greenacre 1965
518	1965 Jul 9	Aristarchus; 2 hr 6 min	Starlike image.	Emanuel	Cameron 1965
519	1965 Jul 31	Aristarchus	Starlike image.	Welsh	Cameron 1965
520	1965 Aug 2	Aristarchus; ~1 min	Starlike brightening, 4th to 9th mag.	Bornhurst	Cameron 1965
521	1965 Aug 3	Aristarchus; 6 min	Starlike image, 6th to 7th mag.	Bornhurst	Cameron 1965
522	1965 Aug 4	Aristarchus; ~2 min	Starlike image, 6th to 7th mag.	Bornhurst	Cameron 1965
523	1965 Sep 2	SE of Ross D	Ridge obscured.	Harris	Harris 1967
524	1965 Sep 8, 13h 20m	Aristarchus	Orange-red strip on floor.	Pressson	Contrib. by Moore
525	1965 Oct 10, 06h 05m	Aristarchus	Pale violet radiance; whole of W interior: dark violet, nimbus, pale violet on plateau.	Bartlett	Bartlett 1967
526	1965 Oct 11, 03h 37m	Aristarchus	Whole crater, exclusive of S area, pale violet; dark violet in nimbus; pale violet on plateau.	Bartlett	Bartlett 1967
527	1965 Oct 12, 02h 50m	Aristarchus	Nimbus only, dark violet hue.	Bartlett	Bartlett 1967

No.	Date and Time	Feature or Location; Duration	Description	Observer	Reference
528	1965 Oct 13, 05h02m	Aristarchus	Pale, blue-violet tint on E wall bright spot and whole length of E wall; pale violet radiance in crater, exclusive of S region. Dark violet stories.	Bartlett	Bartlett 1967
529	1965 Nov 15	Aristarchus	Bright spots.	L. Johnson	Phys. Today 1966
530	1965 Dec 1		Reddish glow followed by black obscuration.	Everard and others	Gingerich 1966
531	1965 Dec 4, 04h25m	Ross D	Obscuration of part of rim, also bright area 7-10 km diameter, not seen on following night (05h06m – 05h30m).	Cross (Harris, Cragg on Dec 5)	Harris 1967
532	1966 Feb 7, 01h10m	Aristarchus	Nimbus only intense violet hue.	Bartlett	Bartlett 1967
533	1966 Mar 29, 21h00m	Archimedes	Floor bands brilliant.	E. G. Hill	B.A.A. Lunar Sec. Circ. 1966, 1, No. 5
534	1966 Apr 2, 23h30m	Aristarchus; 20 min	Central peak very bright.	M. Brown	B.A.A. Lunar Sec. Circ. 1966, 1, No. 7
535	1966 Apr 3, 23h40m	Aristarchus; 20 min	Central peak very bright.	M. Brown	B.A.A. Lunar Sec. Circ. 1966, 1, No. 7
536	1966 Apr 12, 01h05m	Gassendi; 18 min	Abrupt flash of red settling immediately to point of red haze near NW wall. Continuous until 01h23m.	Whippey	B.A.A. Lunar Sec. Circ. 1967, 2, No. 5
537	1966 Apr 30–May 2	Gassendi	Red glows.	Sartory, Moore, Moseley, Ringsdore	J.B.A.A. 1968; B.A.A. Lunar Sec. Circ. 1966, 1, No. 6
538	1966 May 1, 21h50m – 22h45m	Aristarchus; 50 min	Red patch.	Patterson	B.A.A. Lunar Sec. Circ. 1966, 1, No. 6
539	1966 May 1, 22h10m	Aristarchus; 15 min	Small intense white spot NW of crater wall.	M. Brown, Sartory	B.A.A. Lunar Sec. Circ. 1966, 1, Nos. 6, 7
540	1966 May 27, 21h10m	Alphonsus; 50 min	Faint red patches.	Sartory, Moore, Moseley	B.A.A. Lunar Sec. Circ. 1966, 1, No. 6

No.	Date and Time	Feature or Location; Duration	Description	Observer	Reference
541	1966 May 30, 20h52m	Gassendi; 7 min	Blink, orange patch and obscuration.	Sartory	B.A.A. Lunar Sec. Circ. 1966, 1, No. 6
542	1966 Jun 1, 03h20m	Aristarchus	Entire sunlit area of floor, bluish.	Bartlett	Bartlett 1967
543	1966 Jun 3, 06h10m	Aristarchus	Nimbus only, violet hue.	Bartlett	Bartlett 1967
544	1966 Jun 20, 04h30m – 04h40m	Alphonsus; 10 min	Absorption band (4880 ± 50 Å) seen in spectrum of central peak.	Harris, Arriola	Harris 1967
545	1966 Jun 27	Plato; 15 min	Inside SW wall of crater, blink.	Bodley-Robinson, Sartory	B.A.A. Lunar Sec. Circ. 1966, 1, No. 11
546	1966 Jul 10, 02h06m	Triesnecker; 1 hr	Bright streak in crater.	Allen	B.A.A. Lunar Sec. Circ. 1966, 1, No. 10
547	1966 Aug 4-5 23h37m – 23h36m and 02h32m – 02h58m	Plato; 53 min, 26 min	Red color, NE wall and floor.	Corvan, Moseley	B.A.A. Lunar Sec. Circ. 1966, 1, No. 10
548	1966 Sep 2, 00h08m	Gassendi; 3 hr	Reddish patches.	Moore, et al. (8 observers)	B.A.A. Lunar Sec. Circ. 1966, 1, No. 10; Ibid 1966, 1, No. 11
549	1966 Sep 2, 03h16m	Alphonsus; intermittent; 1 hr 02 min	A series of weak glows; final flash observed at 04h18m.	Whipper	B.A.A. Lunar Sec. Circ. 1967, 2, No. 12
550	1966 Sep 2, 03h47m	Gassendi	Blinks on NE, ENE walls and SW and W of central peak.	Moseley	B.A.A. Lunar Sec. Circ. 1966, 1, No. 10
551	1966 Sep 25, 20h29m	Gassendi; 30 min	Reddish patches.	Moore, Moseley	B.A.A. Lunar Sec. Circ. 1966, 1, No. 11
552	1966 Sep 25, 23h12m	Plato; 3 min	Blinks in crater.	Moseley	B.A.A. Lunar Sec. Circ. 1966, 1, No. 11
553	1966 Oct 25, 03h36m	SE of Ross D	Large bright areas obscuring half of crater wall. Not present Oct 21. Newtonian 19"f/7.	Cross	Harris 1967
554	1966 Oct 25, 22h50m	Gassendi	Red blinks, N wall.	Moore, Moseley, Sartory	B.A.A. Lunar Sec. Circ. 1967, 2, No. 1

No.	Date and Time	Feature or Location; Duration	Description	Observer	Reference
555	1966 Oct 29, 00h43m–01h26m	Copernicus, N rim; 45 min	Red spot.	Walker	Walker 1966
556	1966 Dec 22, 06h00m–06h30m	Messier; W. H. Pickering; 30 min	Blinks on floors of both craters.	Kelsey	B.A.A. Lunar Sec. Circ. 1967, 2, No. 1
557	1966 Dec 25, 05h15m–07h10m	Plato; 55 min	Numerous bright streaks on floor, three bright spots on floor, all showed blinks.	Kelsey	B.A.A. Lunar Sec. Circ. 1965, 2, No. 1
558	1966 Dec 25, 06h26m–07h05m	Gassendi; 35 min	Very faint blink on SW floor and another N of it on NW floor (observer considers observation very suspect).	Kelsey	B.A.A. Lunar Sec. Circ. 1967, 2, No. 1
559	1967 Jan 24, 19h35m	Gassendi	Small blink and suspect faint colored patch in outer W wall in position of original observation of 1966 Apr 30.	Sartory, Moore, Moseley, Duckworth, Kilburn	B.A.A. Lunar Sec. Circ. 1967, 2, No. 2 Ibid. 1967, 2, No. 4
560	1967 Feb 17, 17h47m–18h42m	Alphonsus; 25 min	Blink just inside the SW floor of crater suspected on elevation SW of dark patch.	Moore, Moseley	B.A.A. Lunar Sec. Circ. 1967, 2, No. 4
561	1967 Feb 19, 20h30m–20h46m	Alphonsus; 16 min	Bright red glow in position of suspected blink of 1967 Feb 17. Fading by 20h37m.	Moseley, Moore	B.A.A. Lunar Sec. Circ. 1967, 2, No. 4
562	1967 Mar 22, 19h46m	Gassendi	Red color and blink.	Moseley	B.A.A. Lunar Sec. Circ. 1967, 2, No. 5
563	1967 Mar 23, 18h40m	Gassendi	Red color under S wall.	Sartory, Parrant	B.A.A. Lunar Sec. Circ. 1967, 2, No. 5
564	1967 Mar 23, 19h45m	Cobrahead	Red color outside SE wall.	Moore, Moseley, Parrant	B.A.A. Lunar Sec. Circ. 1967, 2, No. 6
565	1967 Mar 23, 19h05m–19h55m	Aristarchus	Red glow.	Sartory, Moore, Moseley, Parrant	B.A.A. Lunar Sec. Circ. 1967, 2, Nos. 5, 6

No.	Date and Time	Feature or Location; Duration	Description	Observer	Reference
566	1967 Apr 15, 19h42m – 21h00m	Aristarchus (on dark side); 1 hr 45 min	Aristarchus very bright. Seeing very good until 21h00m UT, after which seeing too bad to continue observing. On April 16 and 17 nothing special was to be seen.	Classen	Bopmann 1967
567	Apr 21, 19h16m – 21h15m	Aristarchus; 1 hr 59 min	Bright points on S wall. Red patch to NE.	Darnell, Farrant	B.A.A. Lunar Sec. Circ. 1967, 2, No. 7
568	1967 Apr 21, 21h26m	Schroter's Valley, Cobrahead	Red color.	Darnell, Farrant	B.A.A. Lunar Sec. Circ. 1967, 2, No. 7
569	1967 Apr 22	Aristarchus (on bright side)	Aristarchus so bright that it could be seen with the naked eye.	Classen	Bopmann 1967
570	1967 May 20, 20h15m and 21h20m	Aristarchus; 15 min	Red spots on south rim. Moon low.	Darnell	B.A.A. Lunar Sec. Circ. 1967, 2, No. 8
571	1967 May 20	Gassendi	Elongated blink in crater, SW part of floor.	Kelsey	B.A.A. Lunar Sec. Circ. 1967, 2, No. 8
572	1967 May 22, 00h40m – 02h25m	Aristarchus; 45 min	Red-brown color.	C. A. Anderson	B.A.A. Lunar Sec. Circ. 1967, 2, No. 8
573	1967 Jun 18, 22h10m – 22h30m and 23h50m	Gassendi; 1 hr 20 min and 1 hr 9 min	Faint redness outside the SW and SW wall of Gassendi.	Whipsey	B.A.A. Lunar Sec. Circ. 1967, 2, No. 8
574	1967 Aug 15, 21h00m	Alphonsus; 15 min	Glow in interior of crater.	Horowitz	B.A.A. Lunar Sec. Circ. 1967, 2, No. 10
575	1967 Sep 11, 00h32m	Mare Tranquillitatis; 8-9 sec	Black cloud surrounded by violet color.	Montreal group	B.A.A. Lunar Sec. Circ. 1967, 2, No. 12
576	1967 Sep 11, 00h42m	Sabine	Bright yellow flash visible a fraction of a second.	Mrs. P. Jean & Montreal group	B.A.A. Lunar Sec. Circ. 1967, 2, No. 12
577	1967 Sep 7, 02h05m	Aristarchus	Red color observed.	DeLuso	Kelsey 1967

158 IS SOMEONE ON THE MOON?

No.	Date and Time	Feature or Location; Duration	Description	Observer	Reference
578	1967 Oct 19, 02ʰ05ᵐ	SE of Ross D	Bright area moved 86 km/hr toward SSE and expanded as contrast reduced.	Harris	Harris 1967
579	1967 Oct 20, 05ʰ06ᵐ	Kepler, Aristarchus	High noon, 19° after full, quieter. Kepler appeared at least one mag brighter than Aristarchus. On Oct 29 and 22 at 05ʰ UT, relative brightness returned to normal.	Classen	Classen 1967

[1] See text for critique of reports believed to be doubtful.
[2] Deduced from available data.
[3] Probable eastern European or Berlin time.
[4] Berlin time.
[5] Observer (permanent record made).
[6] Pseudonym.

REFERENCES

Alter, D., 1956, Pub. A.S.P., 69, 158.
Alter, D., 1959, Proc. Lunar Plan. Explor. Colloq., 1, part 4, p. 19.
Alter, D., NASA Report.
Argelander, F., 1826, Astr. Nach., 4, 164.
Azevado, R. de, 1962, Lua (Saō Paulo).
Baily, F., 1822, Mem. Astr. Soc., 1, 160.
Barker, R., 1940, Pop. Astr., 48, 19.
Barnard, E. E., 1892, Astr. Nach., 130, No. 3097.
Bartlett, James C., Jr., 1967, Strol. Astr., 20, Nos. 1-2, pp. 24-28.
Baum, R., 1966, private communication to Middlehurst.
Beccaria, G. B., 1781, J. Phys., 17, 447.
Bianchini, F., 1686, Acta Eruditorum, Leipzig.
Birt, W. R., 1864, Astr. Reg., 2, 295.
Birt, W. R., 1869, Astr. Reg., 6, 180.
Birt, W. R., 1870, Astr. Reg., 7, 221.
Bode, J. E., 1788-89, Berlin Mem., p. 204.
Bode, J. E., 1789, Berliner Astr. Jahr., p. 245.
Bode, J. E., 1790, Berliner Astr. Jahr., p. 177.
Bode, J. E., 1792a, Berliner Astr. Jahr., pp. 112, 252.
Bode, J. E., 1792b, Berliner Astr. Jahr., p. 252.
Bode, J. E., 1793, Berliner Astr. Jahr., p. 236.
Bolton, S., 1901, Eng. Mech., 74, 276.
Cameron, W., 1965, private communication to Burley.
Capen, C., 1955, Sky and Tel., 14, 518 (drawing only); private communication to Middlehurst (1967).
Capron, J. Rand, 1879, Aurorae, Their Characters and Spectra (London), p. 71.

REFERENCES

Alter, D., 1956, Pub. A.S.P., 69, 158.
Alter, D., 1959, Proc. Lunar Plan. Explor. Colloq., 1, part 4, p. 19.
Alter, D., NASA Report.
Argelander, F., 1826, Astr. Nach., 4, 164.
Azevado, R. de, 1962, Lua (Sao Paulo).
Baily, F., 1822, Mem. Astr. Soc, 1, 160.

Barker, R., 1940, Pop. Astr., 48, 19.
Barnard, E. E., 1892, Astr. Nach., 130, No. 3097.
Bartlett, James C, Jr., 1967, Strol. Astr., 20, Nos. 1-2, pp. 24-28. Baum, R., 1966, private communication to Middlehurst.

Beccaria, G. B., 1781, J. PJiys., 17, 447.
Bianchini, F., 1686, Acta Eruditorum, Leipzig.
Birt, W. R., 1864, Astr. Reg., 2, 295.
Birt, W. R., 1869, Astr. Reg., 6, 180.
Birt, W. R., 1870, Astr. Reg., 7, 221.
Bode, J. E., 1788-89, Berlin Mem., p. 204.
Bode, J. E., 1789, Berliner Astr. Jahr., p. 245.
Bode, J. E., 1790, Berliner Astr. Jahr., p. 177.
Bode, J. E., 1792a, Berliner Astr. Jahr., pp. 112, 252.
Bode, J. E., 17926, Berliner Astr. Jahr., p. 252.
Bode, J. E., 1793, Berliner Astr. Jahr., p. 236.
Bolton, S., 1901, Eng. Mech., 74, 276.
Cameron, W., 1965, private communication to Burley.
Capen, C, 1955, Sky and Tel., 14, 518 (drawing only); private communication to Middlehurst (1967). Capron, J. Rand, 1879, Aurorae, Their Characters and Spectra (London), p. 71.

Caroche, N. S., 1799, Connaissance des Temps, p. 457. Charbonneaux, M., 1902, Bull. Soc. Astr. France, 16, 14. Chevremont, 1898, Bull. Soc. Astr. France, 12, 97. Classen, J., 1967, private communication to J. Hopmann. Delmotte, G., private communication to Moore.

Denning, W. F., Telescopic Work, p. 121.

Douillet, E., 1933, Bull. Soc. Astr. France, 47, 265.

Elger, T. G. E., 1868, Astr. Reg., 5, 114.

Ellison, W. F. A., 1917, Eng. Meek., 105, 10.

Emmett, R. B., 1826, Ann. Phil., 12, 81; 1929, J. Cliein. Phys., 55, 445; 1826, Bull. Sci. Math. Astr., Phys. et Chiin., 6, 275.

Fallows, T., 1822, Phil. Trans. R. Soc. London, 112, p. 237.
Fauth, P., 1899, Astr. Nach., 151, No. 3614, p. 219.
Fauth, P., 1907, Mitt. Verein. Freund. Astr. Kos. Phys., 17, 13.
Firsoff, V. A., 1962 ed., Strange World of the Moon (New York: Basic Books). Firsoff, V. A., 1966, private communication to Middlehurst.

Fisher, W. J., 1924, "The Brightness of Lunar Eclipses, 1860-1922," Harvard Reprint No. 7. Flammarion, C, 1884, Les Terres du del (Paris: Marpon et Flammarion).
Flaugergues, L., 1822, Corr. astr,, geog., hydrog. et statist., 7, 235.
Fock, A., 1920, Astr. Nach., 210, 293.

Franks, W. S., 1912, Observing book.
Gaudibert, C, 1880, Selenographical J., 3, 28.
Gauss, C. F., 1874, Werke, 6, 436.
Gerling, C. L., 1845, Astr. Nach., 22, 356.
Gingerich, O., 1966, private communication to Middlehurst. Gobel, D. W., 1826, Astr. Nach., 4, 295.

46

Goodacre, W., 1931, *The Moon* (Bournemouth, England: Pardy and Son), p. 246.

Grainger, J. F., and Ring, J., 1963, *Mon. Not. Roy. Astron. Soc.*, 125, 101.

Green, J., 1965, *Ann. N. Y. Acad. Sci.*, 123, 458-465.

Greenacre, J. C., 1963, *Sky and Tel.*, 26, 316.

Greenacre, J. C., 1965, private communication to Middlehurst.

Grover, C., 1866, *Astr. Reg.*, 3, 253.

Gruithuisen, F. von P., 1824, *Archiv. Gesam. Naturl.*, 2, 293 = 1826, *Astr. Nach.*, 4, 205.

Haas, W. H., 1942, *J. Roy. Astr. Soc. Canada*, 36, 237.

Haas, W. H., 1957, *Strol. Astr.*, 11, 133.

Haas, W. H., 1965, private communication to Middlehurst.

Halley, E., 1715, *Phil. Trans. R. Soc. London*, 29, p. 249.

Harris, D. H., 1967, private communication to Middlehurst.

Harrison, J. C., 1876, *Description of England*, ed. Furnivall (New Shakespere Society).

Hart, R., 1855, *Mon. Not. Roy. Astron. Soc.*, 15, 89.

Herschel, W., 1787, *Phil. Trans. R. Soc. London*, 77, 229.

Herschel, W., 1912, *Collected Scientific Papers*, ed. J. L. E. Dreyer (London: Royal Society and the Royal Astronomical Society).

Hess, W., 1911, *Himmels - und Naturerscheinungen in Einblattdrucken des 15 bis 18 Jahrhunderts* (Leipzig).

Hill, S. J., 1966, private communication to Middlehurst.

Hodgson, R., 1848, *Mon. Not. Roy. Astron. Soc.*, 8, 55.

Hodgson, R., 1866, *Astr. Reg.*, 3, 224.

Hole, G. A., 1959, *J. Int. Lunar Soc.*, 1, 90.

Hopmann, J., 1966, private communication to Middlehurst.

Hopmann, J., 1967, private communication to Middlehurst.

Houdard, G., 1917, *Bull. Soc. Astr. France*, 30, 381, 383.

Houzeau, J. C., 1882, *Vade-Mecum d'Astronomie* (Brussels: F. Hayez).

Goodacre, W., 1931, The Moon (Bournemouth, England: Pardy and Son), p. 246. Grainger, J. F., and Ring, J., 1963, Mon. Not. Roy. Astron. Soc, 125, 101. Green, J., 1965, Ann. N. Y. Acad. Sci., 123, 458-465.
Greenacre, J. C, 1963, Sky and Tel., 26, 316.

Greenacre, J. C, 1965, private communication to Middlehurst.

Grover, C., 1866, Astr. Reg., 3, 253.

Gruithuisen, F. von P., 1824, Areliiv. Gesam. Naturl., 2, 293 = 1826, Astr. Nach., 4, 295.

Haas, W. H., 1942, J. Roy. Astr. Soc. Canada, 36, 237.

Haas, W. H., 1957, Strol. Astr., 11, 133.

Haas, W. H., 1965, private communication to Middlehurst.

Halley, E., 1715, Phil. Trans. R. Soc. London, 29, p. 249.

Harris, D. H., 1967, private communication to Middlehurst.

Harrison, J. C, 1876, Description of England, ed. Furnivall (New Shakespere Society).

Hart, R., 1855, Mon. Not. Roy. Astron. Soc, 15, 89.

Herschel, W., 1787, Phil. Trans. R. Soc. London, 77, 229.

Herschel, W., 1912, Collected Scientific Papers, ed. J. L. E. Dreyer (London: Royal Society and the Royal Astronomical Society).

Hess, W., 1911, Himmels - mid Natnrerscheinungen in Einblattdrucken des 15 his 18 Jahrlutnderts (Leipzig).

Hill, S. J., 1966, private communication to Middlehurst. Hodgson, R., 1848, Mon. Not. Roy. Astron. Soc, 8, 55. Hodgson, R., 1866, Astr. Reg., 3, 224.
Hole, G. A., 1959, J. Int. Lunar Soc, 1, 90.

Hopmann, J., 1966, private communication to Middlehurst.
Hopmann, J., 1967, private communication to Middlehurst.
Houdard, G., 1917, Bull. Soc. Astr. France, 30, 381, 383.
Houzeau, J. C, 1882, Vade-Mecum d'Astronomie (Brussels: F. Hayez).

Houzeau, J. C., and Lancaster, A., 1964 ed., *Bibliographie Général d'Astronomie*, ed. D. Dewhirst (2nd ed.; London: Holland Press Ltd.), Vol. II.

Ingall, H., 1864, *Astr. Reg.*, 2, 264.

Jackson, G., 1913, *Bull. Soc. Astr. France*, 27, 262.

Jackson, W. E., 1890-91, *J. Brit. Astr. Assoc.*, 1, 463.

Johnson, S. J., 1877, *Eclipses Past and Future* (London).

Johnson, S. J., 1882, *Astr. Reg.*, 20, 16.

Josselyn, J., 1675, *An Account of Two Voyages to New England* (London), p. 53 (2nd ed., 1865, p. 45).

Joulia, E., 1931, *Bull. Soc. Astr. France*, 45, 149.

Kater, H., 1821, *Phil. Trans. R. Soc. London*, 111, 130.

Kelsey, H. W., 1967, unpublished.

Klado, T. N., 1965, *NASA Tech. Trans. No. F310* (from *Istoriko-astronomicheskiye Issledovaniya*, 6, 1, 1961).

Klein, H., 1879, reported in *Nature*, 20, 462.

Klein, H., 1902, *Pop. Astr.*, 10, 57.

Klein, H., *Wochens. für Astr.*, 42, 364.

Kopal, Z., and Rackham, T. W., 1964a, *Nature*, 201, 238.

Kopal, Z., and Rackham, T. W., 1964b, *Sky and Tel.*, 27, 140.

Kozyrev, N. A., 1957, *Izv. Crim. Astr. Obs.*, 16, 148-161.

Kozyrev, N. A., 1959, *Priroda*, 3, 84.

Kozyrev, N. A., 1962, in *The Moon* (I.A.U. Symposium No. 14) eds. Z. Kopal and Z. Mikhailov (London and New York: Academic Press).

Kozyrev, N. A., 1963, *Nature*, 198, 979.

Krueger, A., 1889, *Astr. Nach.*, 122, 263.

Lalande, J. de, 1792, *L'Astronomie* (Paris; reprint 1966, Johnson Reprint Corp., New York and London).

LeRoy, T., 1912, *Bull. Soc. Astr. France*, 26, 248.

Liais, E., 1865, *L'Espace Céleste*, pp. 143-144 (Paris).

Houzeau, J. C, and Lancaster, A., 1964 ed., Bibliographie General d'Astronomie, ed. D. Dewhirst (2nd ed.; London: Holland Press Ltd.), Vol. II.

Ingall, H., 1864, Astr. Reg., 2, 264.

Jackson, G., 1913, Bull. Soc. Astr. France, 27, 262.

Jackson, W.E.,1890-91, J. Brit.Astr. Assoc,1, 463.

Johnson, S. J., 1877, Eclipses Past and Future (London).

Johnson, S. J., 1882, Astr. Reg., 20, 16.

Josselyn, J., 1675, An Account of TiVo Voyages to Neiv England (London), p. 53 (2nd ed., 1865, p. 45).

Joulia, E., 1931, Bull. Soc. Astr. France, 45, 149.

Kater, H., 1821, Phil. Trans. R. Soc. Loudon, 111, 130.

Kelsey, H. W., 1967, unpublished.

Klado, T. N., 1965, NASA Tech. Trans. No. F310 (from Istoriko-astronomischeskiye Issledovaniya, 6, 1, 1961).

Klein, H., 1879, reported in Nature, 20, 462.
Klein, H., 1902, Pop. Astr., 10, 57.
Klein, H., Wochens. far Astr., 32, 364.
Kopal, Z., and Rackham, T. W., 1964a, Nature, 201, 238. Kopal, Z., and Rackham, T. W., 19646, Sky and Tel., 27, 140. Kozyrev, N. A., 1957, Izv. Crim. Astr. Obs., 16. 148-161. Kozyrev, N. A., 1959, Priroda, 3, 84.

Kozyrev, N. A., 1962, in The Moon (I.A.U. Symposium No. 14) eds. Z. Kopal and Z. Mikhailov (London and New York: Academic Press).

Kozyrev, N. A., 1963, Nature, 198, 979.

Krueger, A., 1889, Astr. Nach., 122, 263.

Lalande, J. de, 1792, lAstronomie (Paris; reprint 1966, Johnson Reprint Corp., New York and London).

LeRoy, T., 1912, Bull. Soc. Astr. France, 26, 248.

Liais, E., 1865, l'Espace Celeste, pp. 143-144 (Paris). 48

Louville, J. E. d'A. de, 1715, Mem. Hist. Acad. R. Sci. Paris, pp. 96, 126-7.
Lowes, J. L., 1927, The Road to Xanadu (London: Cambridge Press), pp. 180, 510.
Luthmer, 1824, Berliner Astr. Jahr., p. 242.
Maskelyne, N., 1795, Phil. Trans. R. Soc. London, 85, 435.
Mather, C., 1714, Phil. Trans. R. Soc. London, 29, 65.
Mayemson, A., 1965, letter to J. S. Hall.
Mellish, J. E., 1909, Eng. Mech., No. 2309, 492.
Merlin, A. C. Eliot, 1909, Eng. Mech., No. 2305, 395.
Moore, P. A., 1953, A Guide to the Moon (New York: W. W. Norton Co.), pp. 113, 115.
Moore, P. A., 1963, Survey of the Moon (New York: W. W. Norton Co.), p. 290.
Moore, P. A., 1965, Ann. N. Y. Acad. Sci., 123, 797-802.
Moye, M., 1898, Bull. Soc. Astr. France, 12, 97.
Moye, M., and Russell, S. C., 1905, Observatory, 28, 141.
Niesten, L., 1884, Bull. Brux., 8, 361.
Niesten, L., and Stuyvaert, E., 1898-99, Ciel et Terre, 19, 567.
Olbers, H. W. M., 1822, Mem. Astr. Soc., 1, 156.
Olbers, H. W. M., 1824, Berliner Astr. Jahr., p. 228.
Parschian, J., 1885, l'Astronomie, 4, 69.
Piazzi, G., 1800, Monatliche Correspondenz, 2, 322.
Piazzi, G., 1810, Monatliche Correspondenz, 21, 96.
Pickering, E. C., 1906, Astr. Nach., 16, No. 3966, 91.
Pickering, W. H., 1902, Pop. Astr., 10, 419.
Pickering, W. H., 1903, The Moon (New York: Doubleday and Page), pp. 40 ff and Plate B.
Poppendiek, H. F., and Bond, W. H., 1959, Pub. A.S.P., 71, 233.
Rankin, T., 1847, Brit. Assoc. Rept., 2, 18.
Rawstron, G. O., 1937, Pop. Astr., 45, 291.

Louville, J. E. d'A. de, 1715, Mem. Hist. Acad. R. Sci. Paris, pp. 96, 126-7.
Lowes, J. L., 1927, The Road to Xanadu (London: Cambridge Press), pp. 180, 510. Luthmer, 1824, Berliner Astr. Jahr., p. 242.
Maskelyne, N., 1795, Phil. Trans. R. Soc. London, 85, 435.
Mather, C, 1714, Phil. Trans. R. Soc. London, 29, 65.
Mayemson, A., 1965, letter to J. S. Hall.
Mellish, J. E., 1909, Eng. Mech., No. 2309, 492.

Merlin, A. C. Eliot, 1909, Eng. Mech., No. 2305, 395.
Moore, P. A., 1953, A Guide to the Moon (New York: W. W. Norton Co.), pp. 113, 115. Moore, P. A., 1963, Survey of the Moon (New York: W. W. Norton Co.), p. 290. Moore, P. A., 1965, Ann. N. Y. Acad. Sci., 123, 797-802.
Moye, M., 1898, Bull. Soc. Astr. France, 12, 97.
Moye, M., and Russell, S. C, 1905, Observatory, 28, 141.

Niesten, L., 1884, Bull. Brux., 8, 361.

Niesten, L., and Stuyvaert, E., 1898-99, del et Terre, 19, 567. Olbers, H. W. M., 1822, Mem. Astr. Soc, 1, 156.
Olbers, H. W. M., 1824, Berliner Astr. Jahr., p. 228. Parsehian, J., 1885, VAstronomie, 4, 69.

Piazzi, G., 1800, Monatliche Correspondenz, 2, 322.
Piazzi, G., 1810, Monatliche Correspondenz, 21, 96.
Pickering, E. C, 1906, Astr. Nach., 16, No. 3966, 91.
Pickering, W. H., 1902, Pop. Astr., 10, 419.
Pickering, W. H., 1903, The Moon (New York: Doubleday and Page), pp. 40 ff and Plate B. Poppendiek, H. F., and Bond, W. H., 1959, Pub. A.S.P., 71, 233.

Rankin, T., 1847, Brit. Assoc. Rept., 2, 18. Rawstron, G. O., 1937, Pop. Astr., 45, 291.

Rey, M. H., 1903, Bull. Soc Astr. France, 17, 315. Ricker, C., 1966, Strol. Astr., 19, Nos. 11-12, p. 194. Rozier, 1788, Obs. sur la Phys., 43, 313.
Rozier, 1792, Berliner Astr. Jahr., p. 176.

Rule, N., 1959, letter to B. J. Bok.
Ruppell,1822, Corr.astr., geog., hydrog.etstatist.,7, 251.
Sanduleak, N., and Stock, J., 1965, Pub. A.S.P., 77, No. 457.

Sato, T., 1964, Sky and Tel., 28, 351.
Scarfe, C. D., 1965, Mon. Not. Roy. Astron. Soc, 130, 19.
Schroter, J. H., 1789, Schriften Gesells. Naturf. Freunde (Lilienthal), 9, 206.
Schroter, J. H., 1791, Selenotopographische Fragmente (Gottingen: Joh. Georg Rosenbusch). Schroter, J. H., 1792rt, Schriften Gesells. Naturf. Freunde (Lilienthal), 10, 413.
Schroter, J. H., 17926, Berliner Astr. Jahr., p. 176.
Seyffer, K. F. von, 1789, J. de Savants, p. 51.
Sforza, G. de, 1905, Bull. Soc. Astr. France, 19, 462.
Shorthill, R., 1963, private communication to J. Green.
Smyth, C. P., 1836, Mon. Not. Roy. Astron. Soc, 3, 141.
Spinrad, H., 1964, Icarus, 3, 500.
Stein, R. J., 1959, Sky and Tel., 19, 211.
Stretton, 1794, Phil. Trans. R. Soc London, 84, 429.

Struve, F. G. W. von, 1323, Astr. Nach., 1, 138. Stuart, L., 1957, J. Int. Lunar Soc, 1.
Tempel, E. W. L., 1867, Astr. Nach., 69, 365. Thornton, F. H., 1947, J. Brit. Astr. Assoc, 57, 143. Thury, M., 1889«, Bull. Astr., 6, 461.

Thury, M., 1889/;, Nature, 41, 183.

Treanor, P., and O'Connell, D. J. K., 1965, private communication to Middlehurst.

Trouvelot, E. L., 1882, The Trouvelot Astronomical Drawings Manual (New York: Scribner and Sons), p. 49.

Ulloa, G. de, 1779, Phil. Trans. R. Soc. London, 69, p. 105; see also, J. Phys., 1780, 15, 319.

Valier, M., 1912, Astr. Nach., 191, 443.

Walker, R. C., 1966, Letter to J. Ashbrook.

Ward, J. T., 1822, Mem. Astr. Soc., 1, 159.

Ward, J. T., 1906-07, J. Brit. Astr. Assoc., 17, 32.

Webb, T. W., 1962 ed., Celestial Objects for Common Telescopes (New York: Dover Publications, Inc.), Vol. I, "The Solar System," edited by M. W. Mayall.

Wilkins, H. P., 1944, J. Brit. Astr. Assoc., 54, 161.

Wilkins, H. P., 1945, J. Brit. Astr. Assoc., 56, 12.

Wilkins, H. P., 1954, Our Moon (London: F. Miller).

Wilkins, H. P., 1958, J. Int. Lunar Soc., 1, 76.

Wilkins, H. P., 1959, Mon. Not. Roy. Astron. Soc., 119, 421.

Wilkins, H. P., and Moore, P. A., 1953, The Moon (London: Faber and Faber, Ltd.).

Wilkins, W., 1794, Phil. Trans. R. Soc. London, 84, 429.

Williams, A. S., 1882, Selenographical J., 5, 36.

Williams, W. O., 1867, Astr. Reg., 4, 14.

Wullerstorff, M., 1846, in Annuaire du Bureau des Longitudes pour 1846, p. 364.

Zach, F. X. de, 1822, Corr. astr. géog., hydrog. et statist., 7, 235.

Zantedeschi, Abbé, 1846, in Annuaire du Bureau des Longitudes pour 1846, p. 364.

Journals

Astr. Reg., 1864, 2, 264.

Astr. Reg., 1866, 3, 189, 252.

Astr. Reg., 1868, 5, 220.

Treanor, P., and O'Connell, D. J. K., 1965, private communication to Middlehurst.

Trouvelot, E. L., 1882, The Trouvelot Astronomical Drawings Manual (New York: Scribner and Sons), p. 49.

Ulloa, G. de, 1779, Phil. Trans. R. Soc. London, 69, p. 105; see also, J. Pliys., 1780, 15, 319. Valier, M., 1912, Astr. Nach., 191, 443.

Walker, R. C, 1966, Letter to J. Ashbrook.
Ward, J. T., 1822, Mem. Astr. Soc., 1, 159.

Ward, J. T., 1906-07, J. Brit. Astr. Assoc, 17, 32.

Webb, T. W., 1962 ed., Celestial Objects for Common Telescopes (New York: Dover Publications, Inc.), Vol. I, "The Solar System," edited by M. W. Mayall.

Wilkins, H. P., 1944, J. Brit. Astr. Assoc, 54, 161.
Wilkins, H. P., 1945, J. Brit. Astr. Assoc, 56, 12.
Wilkins, H. P., 1954, Our Moon (London: F. Miller).
Wilkins, H. P., 1958, J. Int. Lunar Soc, 1, 76.
Wilkins, H. P., 1959, Mon. Not. Roy. Astron. Soc, 119, 421.
Wilkins, H. P., and Moore, P. A., 1958, The Moon (London: Faber and Faber, Ltd.). Wilkins, W., 1794, Phil. Trans. R. Soc. Lottdon, 84, 429.

Williams, A. S., 1882, Selenographical J., 5, 36.
Williams, W. O., 1867, Astr. Reg., 4, 14.
Wullerstorff, M., 1846, in Annuaire du Bureau des Longitudes pour 1846, p. 364.

Zach, F. X. de, 1822, Corr. astr. ge'og., hydrog. et statist., 7, 235.
Zantedeschi, Abbe, 1846, in Annuaire du Bureau des Longitudes pour 1846, p. 364.

Journals

Astr. Reg., 1864, 2, 264. Astr. Reg., 1866, 3, 189, 252. Astr. Reg., 1868, 5, 220.

Astr. Reg., 1882, 20, 165.
l'Astronomie, (old series) 4, 227. l'Astronomie, 1885, p. 212.
l'Astronomie, 1889, pp. 235, 275. l'Astronomie, 9, 149.
l'Astronomie, 11, 33.
l'Astronomie, 13, 34.
B.A.A. Lunar Sec. Circ, 1966, i, No. 6.

B.A.A. Lunar Sec. Circ, 1966, 1, No. 7.
B.A.A. Lunar Sec. Circ, 1966, i, No. 8.
B.A.A. Lunar Sec. Circ, 1966, 1, No. 10. S.A.A. Lunar Sec. Circ, 1966, i, No. 11. B.A.A. Lunar Sec. Circ, 1966, 1, No. 12. B.A.A. Lunar Sec. Circ, 1967, 2, No. 1.
B.A.A. L/mar Sec. Circ, 1967, 2, No. 3.
B.A.A. Lunar Sec. Circ, 1967, 2, No. 4.
B.A.A. Lunar Sec. Circ, 1967, 2, No. 7.
B.A.A. Lunar Sec. Circ, 1967, 2, No. 8.
B.A.A. Lunar Sec Circ, 1967, 2, No. 10. B.A.A. Lunar Sec. Circ, 1967, 2, No. 12. B.A.A. Mem., 1895, 5, 3rd Report, Lunar Section. B.A.A. Mem., 1898, 6, 4th Report, Lunar Section. B.A.A. Mem., 1916, 20, 7th Report, Lunar Section. B.A.A. Rept., 1871, p. 88.

Bull. Soc Astr. France, 1903, 17, pp. 205, 315, 447. Eng. Mech., 1882, 25, 89, 335, 432.

Eng. Mech., 28, 725.
Eng. Mech., 101, pp. 28, 47.
Eng. Mech., 103, 10.
Eng. Mech., 109, 517.
Hemel en Dampkring, 1967, 3, 66.
Hesperi et Phosphori Phaenomena, 1728, Rome.
J. Brit. Astr. Assoc., 1948, 58, 171.
J. Brit. Astr. Assoc., 1949, 59, 250.
J. Brit. Astr. Assoc., 1955, 65, 189.
J. Brit. Astr. Assoc., 1956, 66, 258.
J. Brit. Astr. Assoc., 1966, 77(1), 47.
J. Int. Lunar Soc., 1960, 1, 144.
Knowledge, 7, 224.
Mon. Not. Roy. Astron. Soc., 1848, 8, 130, 162.
l'Opinione Nazionale, March 3, 1877.
Phil. Trans. R. Soc. London, 1739, 41, p. 228.
Physics Today, 1966, 19, 98.
Popular Astronomy, 1894-95, 2.
Popular Astronomy, 1902, 10, 67.
Popular Astronomy, 1932, 10, 316.
Proc. Liverpool Astr. Soc., 1883, 1, 31, 32.
Rept. Brit. Assoc., 1871.
Revista Astronomica, 1965, 36, 159.
Sci. Amer., 1882, 46, 49.
Sci. Amer., 1919, 121, 181.
Sci. Amer. Suppl., 7, 2629.

Eng. Mech., 28, 725.
Eng. Mech., 101, pp. 28, 47.
Eng. Mech., 103, 10.
Eng. Mech., 109, 517.
Hemel en Dampkring, 1967, 5, 66.
Hesperi et Phosphori Phaenomena, 1728, Rome.

J. Brit. Astr. Assoc, 1948, 58, 171. J. Brit. Astr. Assoc, 1949, 59, 250.
J. Brit. Astr. Assoc, 1955, (55, 189. J. Brit. Astr. Assoc, 1956, 66, 258.
J. Bra'*. Astr. Assoc, 1966, "(1), 47. J. Int. Lunar Soc, 1960, 1, 144.

Knowledge, 7, 224.
Mo??. Afe/;. Rov. Astron. Soc, 1848, S, 130, 162. I'Opinioite Nazionale, March 3, 1877.
Phil. Trans. R. Soc. London, 1739, 41, p. 228. Physics Today, 1966, 19, 98. PopularAstronomy, 1894-95, 2.
Popular Astronomy, 1902, iO, 67.
Popular Astronomy, 1932, 40, 316.
Proc. Liverpool Astr. Soc, 1883, i, 31, 32. Rept. Brit. Assoc, 1871.
Revista Astronomica, 1965, 56", 159.
Sci. Amer., 1882, J6, 49.
Sci. Amer., 1919, i-27, 181.
Sci. Amer. Suppl., 7, 2629.

Selenographical J., 1878, 1, 7, 27. Selenographical J., 1880, 3, 60.
Shins, 1878, 11, 260.
Siriits, 1879, i.2, 20.

Sn-ms, 1881, 14, 68. Sims, 1882, 15, 167. Sinas, 1883, 2 6, 279. Siriits, 1884, 2 7, 140. Siriits, 1885, 2<S 20, 43. Siriits, 1887, 20, 45, 94. Siriits, 1888, 2i, 249. Sims, 1889, 22.

Sirius, 1890, 23.
Siriits, 1892, 25, 213.
Siras, 1895, 28, 92.
S?n'»s, 1896, 2.9, 256.
Sirius, 1897, 50, 50.
Sirius, 1903, 36.
SA'.v fi»wf Telescope, 1955, 75, 45.
S/?v and Telescope, 1964, 27, 3 (article by L. J. Robinson). Strolling Astronomer, 1951, 5,8.
Strolling Astronomer, 1955, 5,22-23, 130.
Strolling Astronomer, 1956, 20, 42.
Strolling Astronomer, 1959, 23, 95.
Strolling Astronomer, 1962, 26,41.

Strolling Astronomer, 1966, 19, 145-146. The Student, 1, 261.

Goddard Space Flight Center
National Aeronautics and Space Administration

Greenbelt, Maryland, November 1, 1967 841-11-78-01-51

NASA-Langley, 1968 30

55

182 IS SOMEONE ON THE MOON?

```
Science qQB 581 .M56
Middlehurst, Barbara M.
Chronological catalog of
   reported lunar events
```

DATE DUE

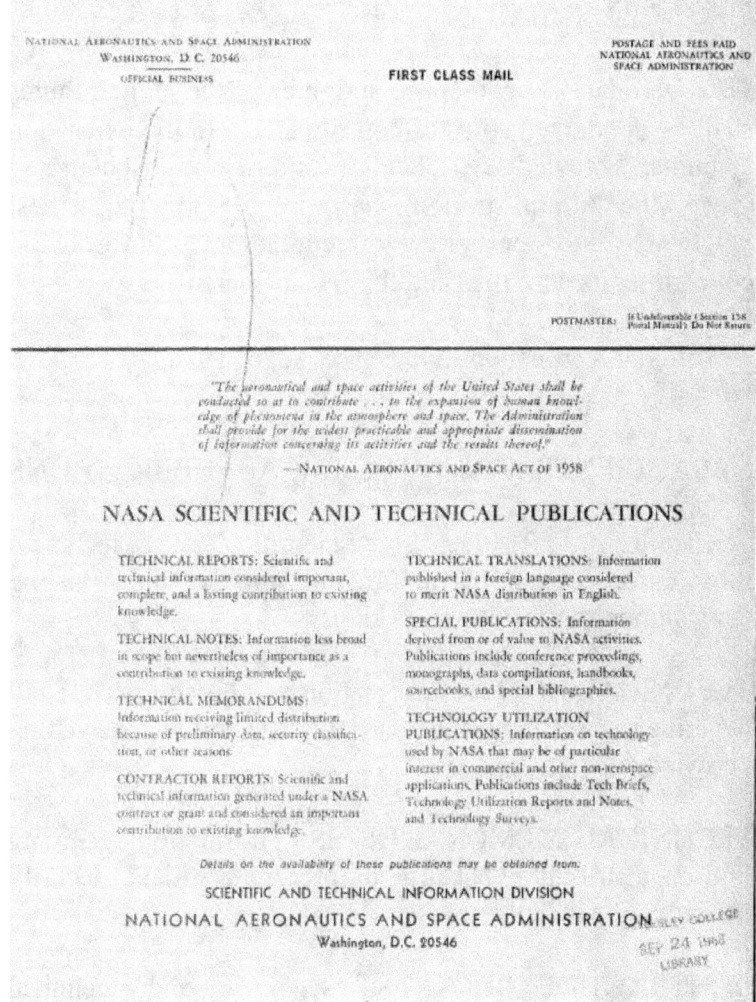

National Aeronautics and Space Administration Washington, D. C. 20546

OFFICIAL BUSINESS

POSTAGE and fees paid national aeronautics and space administration

FIRST CLASS MAIL

"The 'aeronautical and space activities of the United States shall be conducted so as to contribute . . . to the expansion of human knowledge of phenomena in the atmosphere and space, the Administration shall provide for the widest practicable and appropriate dissemination of information concerning its activities and the results thereof!'

—National Aeronautics and Space Act of 1958

NASA SCIENTIFIC AND TECHNICAL PUBLICATIONS

TECHNICAL REPORTS: Scientific and technical information considered important, complete, and a lasting contribution to existing knowledge.

TECHNICAL NOTES: Information less broad in scope but nevertheless of importance as a contribution to existing knowledge.

TECHNICAL MEMORANDUMS: Information receiving limited distribution because of preliminary data, security classification, or other reasons.

CONTRACTOR REPORTS: Scientific and technical information generated under a NASA contract or grant and considered an important contribution to existing knowledge.

TECHNICAL TRANSLATIONS: Information published in a foreign language considered to merit NASA distribution in English.

SPECIAL PUBLICATIONS: Information derived from or of value to NASA activities. Publications include conference proceedings, monographs, data compilations, handbooks, sourcebooks, and special bibliographies.

TECHNOLOGY UTILIZATION PUBLICATIONS: Information on technology used by NASA that may be of particular interest in commercial and other non-aerospace applications. Publications include Tech Briefs, Technology Utilization Reports and Notes, and Technology Surveys.

Details on the availability of these publications may be obtained from: SCIENTIFIC AND TECHNICAL INFORMATION DIVISION

NATIONAL AERONAUTICS AND SPACE
ADMINISTRATION Washington, D.C. 20546

APPENDIX B
OPERATION HORIZON

Of course, the more recent activity sighted on the Moon could be caused by a military presence on the Moon, Attached, are the first few pages of the documents referring to Project Horizon, a plan, approved by the Joint Chiefs of Staff and the President, to put a manned based on the Moon in 1959. The entire declassified project is 116 pages and can be found in a companion volume to this work.

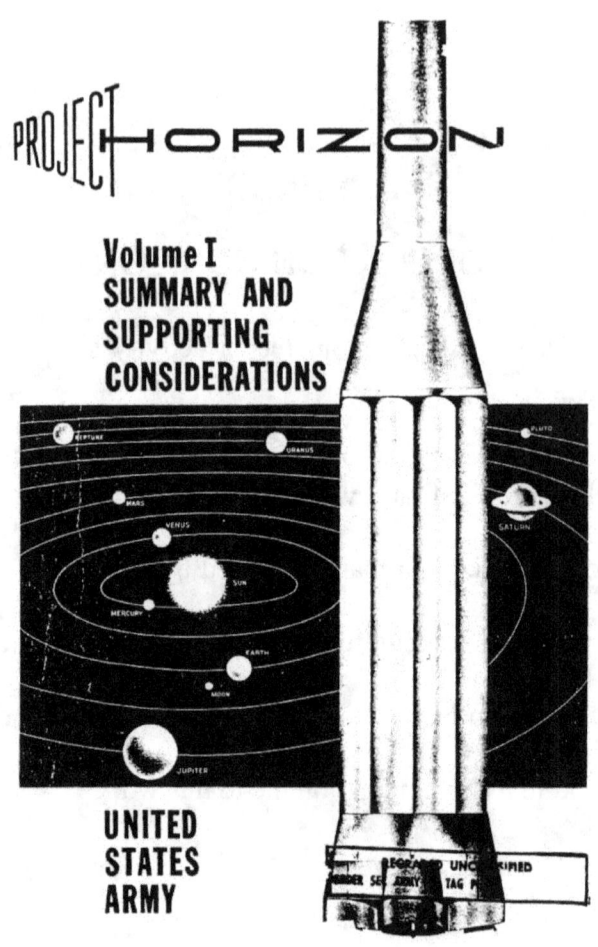

Volume I · SUMMARY AND SUPPORTING CONSIDERATIONS

UNITED STATES ARMY

UNCLASSIFIED

CRD/I (S) Proposal to Establish a Lunar Outpost (C)

Chief of Ordnance   CRD   20 Mar 1959

1. (U) Reference letter to Chief of Ordnance from Chief of Research and Development, subject as above.

2. (C) Subsequent to approval by the Chief of Staff of reference, representatives of the Army Ballistic Missiles Agency indicated that supplementary guidance would be required concerning the scope of the preliminary investigation specified in the reference. In particular these representatives requested guidance concerning the source of funds required to conduct the investigation.

3. (S) I envision expeditious development of the proposal to establish a lunar outpost to be of critical importance to the U. S. Army of the future. This evaluation is apparently shared by the Chief of Staff in view of his expeditious approval and enthusiastic endorsement of initiation of the study. Therefore, the detail to be covered by the investigation and the subsequent plan should be as complete as is feasible in the time limits allowed and within the funds currently available within the office of the Chief of Ordnance. In this time of limited budget, additional monies are unavailable. Current programs have been scrutinized rigidly and identifiable "fat" trimmed away. Thus high study costs are prohibitive at this time.

4. (C) I leave it to your discretion to determine the source and the amount of money to be devoted to this purpose.

Signed
ARTHUR G. TRUDEAU
Lieutenant General, GS
Chief of Research and Development

Regraded Unclassified
by authority of Form DA 1575
dtd 21 Sep 1961
by Lt. Col. Donald E. Simon, CS

CRD/I (S) Proposal to Establish a Lunar Outpost (C)

20 Mar 1959
1. (U) Reference letter to Chief of Ordnance from Chief of Research and

Development, subject as above.

2. (C) Subsequent to approval by the Chief of Staff of reference, representatives of the Army Ballistic Agency indicated that supplementary guidance would be required concerning the scope of the preliminary investigation specified in the reference. In particular these representatives requested guidance concerning the source of funds required to conduct the investigation.

3. (S) I envision expeditious development o! the proposal to establish a lunar outpost to be of critical importance to the p. S. Army of the future. This evaluation is apparently shared by the Chief of Staff in view of his expeditious approval and enthusiastic endorsement of initiation of the study. Therefore, the detail to be covered by the investigation and the subsequent plan should be as complete as is feasible in the tin1e limits allowed and within the funds currently available within the office of the Chief of Ordnance. In this time of limited budget, additional monies are unavailable. Current. programs have been scrutinized rigidly and identifiable "fat" trimmed away. Thus, high study costs are prohibitive at this time,

4. (C) I leave it to your discretion to determine the source and the amount of money to be devoted to this purpose.

Signed
ARTHUR G. TRUDEAU
Lieutenant General, CS
Chief of Research and Development

Regraded Unclassified
by authority--fc);:m-r)A-157'5'"-

dtd 21 Sep 1961
by

Chief of Ordnance

SECRET Draft
UNCLASSIFIED

Requirement for a Lunar Outpost

1. General

There is a requirement for a manned military outpost on the moon. The lunar outpost is required to develop and protect potential United States interests on the moon; to develop techniques in moon-based surveillance of the earth and space, in communications relay, and in operations on the surface of the moon; to serve as a base for exploration of the moon, for further exploration into space and for military operations on the moon if required; and to support scientific investigations on the moon.

2. Operational Concept.

Initially the outpost will be of sufficient size and contain sufficient equipment to permit the survival and moderate constructive activity of a minimum number of personnel (about 10 - 20) on a sustained basis. It must be designed for expansion of facilities, resupply, and rotation of personnel to insure maximum extension of sustained occupancy. It should be designed to be self-sufficient for as long as possible without outside support. In the location and design of the base, consideration will be given to operation of a triangulation station of a moon-to-earth base line space surveillance system, facilitating communications with and observation of the earth, facilitating travel between the moon and the earth, exploration of the moon and further explorations of space, and to the defense of the base against attack if required. The primary objective is to establish the first permanent manned installation on the moon. Incidental to this mission will be the investigation of the scientific, commercial, and military potential of the moon.

3. Background of Requirement.

   a. References:

      (1) NSC policy on outer space.

      (2) OCB Operations Plan on Outer Space.

   b. Reason for Requirement.

      (1) The national policy on outer space includes the objective of development and exploiting US outer space capabilities as needed to achieve scientific, military, and potential purposes. The OCB Operations Plan to implement this policy establishes a specific program to obtain scientific data on space environment out to the vicinity of the moon,

Regraded CONFIDENTIAL
13 March 1963.

1 . General

Requirement for a Lunar Outpost

There is a requirement for a manned outpost on the moon. The lunar outpost is :required to develop and protect potential United States interests on the moon; to develop techniques in moon-based surveil- lance of the earth and space, in relay, and in operations on the surface of the moon; to serve as a base for exploration of the nloon, for further exploration into space and for military operations on the moon if required; and to support scientific investigations on the moon.

2. Operational Concept.

Initially, the outpost will be of sufficient size and contain sufficient equipment to permit the survival and moderate constructive activity of a minimum number of personnel (about 10 - 20) on a sustained basis. It must be designed for expansion of facilities, resupply, and rotation of personnel to insure maximum extension of sustained occupancy. It should be to be self-sufficient for as long as possible without outside support. In the location and design of the base, consideration will be given to operation of a triangulation station of a moon-to-earth base line space surveillance system, facilitating communications with and observation of the earth, facilitating travel between the moon and the earth, exploration of the moon and further explorations of space, and to the defense of the base against attack if required. The primary objective is to establish the first permanent manned installation on the moon. Incidental to this mission will be the investigation of the scientific, commercial, and military potential of the moon.

3. Background of Requirement.

a. References:

(1) NSC policy on

(2) OCB Operations Plan on Outer Space.

b. Reason for Requirement.

(1) 1he national policy on outer includes the objective of development and exploiting US outer space capabilities as needed to achieve scientific, military, and potential purposes. The CCD Operations Plan to implement this policy establishes a specific program to obtain scientific data on space environment out to the vicinity of the moon,

R e g r a d e e l 13

Draft

UNCLASSIFIED

including the moon's gravitational and magnetic fields and to explore the characteristics of the moon's surface. There are no known technical barriers to the establishment of a manned installation on the moon.

(2) The establishment of a manned base of operations on the moon has tremendous military and scientific potential. Because invaluable scientific, military, and political prestige will come to the nation that first establishes a lunar base, it is imperative that the United States be first.

(3) The full extent of the military potential cannot be predicted, but it is probable that observation of the earth and space vehicles from the moon will prove to be highly advantageous. By using a moon-to-earth base line, space surveillance by triangulation promises great range and accuracy. The presently contemplated earth-based tracking and control network will be inadequate for the deep space operations contemplated. Military communications may be greatly improved by the use of a moon-based relay station. The employment of moon-based weapons systems against earth or space targets may prove to be feasible and desirable. Moon-based military power will be a strong deterrent to war because of the extreme difficulty, from the enemy point of view, of eliminating our ability to retaliate. Any military operations on the moon will be difficult to counter by the enemy because of the difficulty of his reaching the moon, if our forces are already present and have means of countering a landing or of neutralizing any hostile forces that has landed. The situation is reversed if hostile forces are permitted to arrive first. They can militarily counter our landings and attempt to deny us politically the use of their property.

(4) The scientific advantages are equally difficult to predict but are highly promising. Study of the universe, of the moon, and of the space environment will all be aided by scientific effort on the moon. Perhaps the most promising scientific advantage is the usefulness of a moon base for further explorations into space. Materials on the moon itself may prove to be valuable and commercially exploitable.

4. Organizational Concept.

The establishment of the outpost should be a special project having authority and priority similar to the Manhattan Project in World War II. Once established, the lunar base will be operated under the control of a unified space command. Space, or certainly that portion of outer space encompassing the earth and the moon, will be considered a military theater. The control of all United States military forces by unified commands is already established and military operations in space should be no exception. A unified space command would control and utilize, besides the lunar base,

2

---

including the moon's gravitational and magnetic fields and to explore the characteristics of the moon's surface. There are no known technical barriers to the establishment of a manned installation on the moon.

(2) The establishment of a manned base of operations on the moon has tremendous military and scientific potential. Because invaluable scientific, military, and political prestige

will come to the nation that first establishes a lunar base, it is imperative that the United States be first.

(3) The full extent of the military potential cannot be predicted, but it is probable that observation of the earth and space vehicles from the moon will. prove to be highly advantageous. By using a moon-to-earth base 1ine, space surveillance by triangulation promises great range and accuracy. 'I'he presently contemplated earth-based tracking and control will be inadequate for the deep space operations contemplated. military communications may be greatly improved by the use of a moon-based relay station. Though employment of moon-based weapons systems against earth or space targets may prove to be feasible and desirable, Moon-based military power will be a deterrent to war because of the extreme difficulty,
from the enemy point of view, of eliminating our ability to retaliate. Any military operations on the moon will be difficult to counter by the enemy because of the difficulty of his reaching the moon, if our forces are already present and have means of countering a landing or of neutralizing any hostile forces that has landed. The situation is reversed if hostile forces arc permitted to arrive first. They can militarily counter our landings and attempt to deny us politically the use of their property.

(4) The scientific advantages arc equally difficult to predict but arc highly promising. Study of the universe, of the moon, and
of the space environment will all be aided by scientific effort on the moon. Perhaps the most promising scientific is the usefulness of a base for furtl1cr explorations into space. Materials on the

moon itself may prove to be valuable and commercially exploitable.

4. Organizational Concept.

'I'he establishment of the outpost should be a special project having authority and priority similar to the Manhattan Project in World War II. Once established, the lunar base be operated under the control of a unified space command. Space or certainly that portion of outer space encompassing the earth and the moon, will be considered a military theater. The control of all United States military forces by unified is already established and military operations in space should be no exception. A unified space command would control and utilize, besides the lunar base,

2

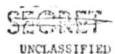

UNCLASSIFIED

operational military satellites and space vehicles, space surveillance systems, and the logistical support thereof. Other space commands might be organized as our operations extended to translunar space.

5. Degree of Urgency.

To be second to the Soviet Union in establishing an outpost on the moon would be disastrous to our nation's prestige and in turn to our democratic philosophy. Although it is contrary to United States policy, the Soviet Union in establishing the first permanent base, may claim the moon or critical areas thereof for its own. Then a subsequent attempt to establish an outpost by the United States might be considered and propagandized as a hostile act. The Soviet Union in propaganda broadcasts has announced the 50th anniversary of the present government (1967) will be celebrated by Soviet citizens on the moon. The National Space policy intelligence estimate is that the Soviets could land on the moon by 1968.

6. Maintenance and Supply Implications.

The maintenance and supply effort to support a lunar base will be high by present standards. Continued delivery of equipment and means of survival will be required and each delivery will be costly. Every conceivable solution for minimizing the logistic effort must be explored. Maximum use of any oxygen or power source on the moon through regenerative or other techniques must be exploited. Means of returning safely to earth must be available to the occupants of the outpost.

7. Training and Personnel Implications.

The number of personnel on the base itself will be quite small, at least initially, but the total number of personnel supporting the effort may be quite large. Until further study is made a realistic qualitative and quantitative personnel estimate cannot be provided. The training requirements of earth based support personnel would resemble those of personnel in long range ballistic missile units and radar tracking systems. For the relatively small number of personnel actually transported to the moon base, training requirements would be exacting in many fields.

8. Additional Items and Requirements.

A complete family of requirements and supporting research and development projects will be necessary to develop all of the supporting equipment to establish a lunar base. Very high thrust boosters, space vehicles, intermediate space stations, space dwellings, clothing and

3

UNCLASSIFIED

operational military satellites and space vehicles, space surveillance systems, and the logistical support thereof. Outer space might be organized
as our operations extended to translunar space.

5. Degree of Urgency.

To be second to the Soviet Union in an outpost on the moon would be disastrous to our nation's prestige and in turn to our democratic philosophy. Although it is contrary to United States policy, the Soviet Union in establishing the first permanent base, may claim the moon or critical areas thereof for its own. Then n subsequent attempt to establish an outpost by the United States might be considered and as a hostile act. The Soviet Union in propaganda broadcasts has announced the 50th anniversary of the present government (1967) will be celebrated by Soviet citizens on the moon. The National Space policy intelligence estimate is that the Soviets could land on the moon by 1968.

6. Maintenance and Supply Implications.

The maintenance and supply effort to support a lunar base will be high by present standards. Continued delivery of equipment and means of survival will be required and each delivery will be costly. Every conceivable solution for the logistic effort must be explored. Maximum use of any oxygen or power source on the moon through regenerative or other techniques must be exploited. Means of returning safely to earth must be available to the occupants of the outpost.

7. Training and Personnel Implications

The number of personnel on the base itself will be quite small, at least initially, but the total number of personnel supporting the effort may be quite large. Until further study is made a realistic and quantitative personnel estimate cannot be provided. The training requirements of earth based support personnel would resemble those of personnel in long range ballistic missile units and radar tracking systems. For the relatively small of personnel actually tral1sported to the moon base, training requirements would be exacting in many fields.

8. Additional Items and Requirements.

A complete family of requirements and supporting research and development projects will be necessary to develop all of the supporting equipment to establish a lunar base. Very high thrust boosters, space vehicles, intermediate space stations, space dwellings, clothing and

UNCLASSIFIED

survival gear to be used on the moon, means of transportation to the moon, and equatorial launching site, tracking equipment and many other developments will be necessary. Eventually concepts of military operations on or in the vicinity of the moon will have to be developed and, from these, supporting requirements for special weapons and equipment will be developed. Research in weapons effects, mapping, and extraction of oxygen, water, and other useful materials from the natural environment will be required.

9. Additional Comments.

a. Two broad problem areas must be considered in meeting the requirement. One is the design, and construction of the outpost. The other is the transportation required to establish and support the outpost.

b. The outpost itself could have one of several forms or be a combination of them. Holes or caves could be covered and sealed with pressure bags. By this means temperature extremes are alleviated and vulnerability to meteorites is lessened. Expansive bags or folding sections could be set on the surface. The rocket transport vehicle itself or used fuel tanks saved for the purpose could be used. Tanks now planned will be from 160" to 256" in diameter. A number of solutions to providing power and sustaining life are possible. By using solar or nuclear power oxygen and water may be extracted from the natural environment should be attainable.

c. The transport could be accomplished either by direct movement by multistage rocket to the moon, or by the use of intermediate orbiting space stations. The first solution imposes enormous power requirements to lift a load of any significance but should not be overlooked. The second solution has promise of early success because it can be accomplished with rocket engines now under development. By the use of vehicles with 1.5 million pound thrust first stage and high energy upper stages significant loads can be placed in orbit and assembled for further travel to the moon and return. Fifteen such vehicles can place enough equipment in orbit to assemble a vehicle approaching 500,000 pounds in weight. A series of 500,000 pound space vehicles is adequate to establish and support the outpost.

4

survival gear to be used on the moon, means of transportation to the moon, and equatorial launching site, tracking equipment and many other developments will be necessary. Eventually concepts of military operations on or in the vicinity of the moon will have to be developed and, from these, supporting requirements for special weapons and oquip1oent will be developed. Research in weapons effects, mapping, and extraction of oxygen, water, and other useful materials from the natural environment will be required.

9. Additional

a. Two broad problem areas must be considered in meeting the requirement. One is the design, and construction of the outpost. The other is the transportation required to establish and support the outpost.

b. The outpost itself could have one of several forms or be a combination of them. Holes or caves could be covered and sealed with pressure bags. By this means temperature extremes are alleviated and vulnerability to meteorites is lessened. Expansive bags or folding sections could be set on the surface. The rocket transport vehicle itself or used fuel tanks saved for the purpose could be used. Tanks now planned will be from 160" to 256" in diameter. A number of solutions to providing power and sustaining life are possible. By using solar or nuclear power oxygen and water may be extracted from the environment should be attainable.

c. The transport could be accomplished either by direct movement by rocket to the moon, or by the of intermediate orbiting space stations. The first solution imposes enormous power requirements to lift n load of any significance but should not be overlooked. The second solution has promise of early success because it can be accomplished with rocket engines now under development. By the use of vehicles with 1.5 million pound thrust first stage and high energy upper stages significant loads can be placed in orbit and assembled for further travel to the moon and return. Fifteen such vehicles can place enough equipment in orbit to assemble a vehicle approaching 500,000 in weight. A series of 500,000 pound space vehicles is adequate to establish and support the outpost.

HEADQUARTERS
DEPARTMENT OF THE ARMY
Office of the Chief of Research and Development
Washington 25, D.C.

20 Mar 1959

SUBJECT: Proposal to Establish a Lunar Outpost (C)

TO: Chief of Ordnance
Department of the Army
Washington 25, D. C.

1. The Army is engaged in determining objectives and requirements for outer space operations. The most challenging and perhaps the most urgent objective is that of establishing a manned lunar outpost on the moon.

2. This lunar base is needed to protect United States interests on the moon, develop techniques in moon-based surveillance of the earth and space, in communications relay, and in operations on the surface of the moon. When established, the lunar station would be utilized as a base for exploration of the moon, for further explorations into space, and for military operations if required. The base is also needed to support scientific investigations on the moon. It is considered of the utmost importance that the moon be first occupied by the U. S. so that the U. S. can deny Soviet territorial, commercial, or technological claims. If a permanent base can be established first by the United States, the prestige and psychological advantage to the nation will be invaluable.

3. You are therefore requested as a matter of urgency to make a preliminary investigation to determine the probable means and techniques of accomplishment and to develop a plan, including estimated time scheduling and costs, for establishing a lunar base by the quickest means possible. The investigation should include a determination of the feasibility of landing a manned vehicle by 1966 and of establishing a permanent base as soon thereafter as possible. This preliminary investigation will be the first of a series of steps to establish a lunar base program and will be used by the General Staff as background information for making a firm proposal to higher authority. If approved, the lunar base program would become a major part of the National Space program.

4. Your investigation will be classified SECRET and will be made known only to those persons required to have knowledge of the project.

Regraded CONFIDENTIAL 13 Mar 1962
(Appropriate Clasisifcation) (Date)

T/F Cy #3

Regraded Unclassified
by authority of Form DA 1575,
dtd 21 Sept. 1961
by LtCol Donald E. Simon, GS

HEADQUARTERS DEPARTMENT OF THE ARMY

Office of the Chief of Research and Development -
Washington 25, D.C.

SUBJECT: Proposal to Establish a Lunar Outpost (C)

TO: Chief of Ordnance Department of the Army

Washington 25 D. C.

1. The Army is engaged in determining objectives and requirements f or outer space operations. The most challenging and perhaps the most urgent objective is that of establishing a manned outpost on the moon.

Urgent

2. This lunar base is needed to protect United States interests on
the moon, develop techniques in moon-based surveillance of the earth and space, in communications relay, and in operations on the surface of the moon. When established, the lunar station would be utilized as a base for exploration of the moon, for further explorations into space, and for military operations if required. The is also needed to support scientific investigations on the moon. It is considered of the utmost importance that the moon be first occupied by the U. S. so that the U. S. can deny Soviet territorial, commercial, or technological claims. If a permanent base can be established first by the United States, the prestige and psychological advantage to the nation will be invaluable .

3. You are therefore requested as a matter of urgency to make a preliminary investigation to determine the probable means and techniques of accomplishment and to develop a plan, including estimated time scheduling and costs, for establishing a lunar by the quickest means possible.

The investigation should include a determination of the feasibility of landing a vehicle by 1966 and of establishing a base as soon thereafter as possible. This preliminary investigation will be the first of a series of steps to establish a lunar base program and will be used by the General Staff as background information for making a firm proposal to higher authority. If approved, the lunar base program would become a major part of the National Space Program.

4. Your investigation will be classified SECRET and will be made known only to persons required to have of knowledge of the project.

No contacts with agencies outside the Army will be made until after the results of the preliminary investigation have been presented to the Department of Defense. The findings of the initial investigation will be made through my office to the Chief of Staff. No additional distribution will be made and no public release will be made concerning this project. Because of the sensitive aspects of this proposal it is essential that this project not be disclosed prematurely.

5. Your plan of accomplishment should include full utilization of the other technical services and combat arms to the extent feasible and necessary. In the accomplishment of this investigation the Chief of Engineers will be responsible for the design, construction, and maintenance of the base and the Chief Signal Officer will be responsible for the communications and other support for which he is peculiarly qualified. Specific emphasis should be given to the Army wide capability to contribute to this project. The results of this preliminary investigation are requested by 15 May 1959.

6. Reproduction of this letter to the extent you deem essential is authorized. All copies will be recorded.

1 incl.

ARTHUR G. TRUDEAU

LIEUTENANT GENERAL, GS

CHIEF OF RESEARCH AND DEVELOPMENT

INDEX

(

(CIG). *See* Counter Intelligence Group
(FOIA). *See* Freedom of Information Request

1

193rd Infantry Brigade. *See* Panama Canal Zone

5

509th Bomber Group. *See* Roswell Army Airfield

A

Aldrin, Buzz, 12, 14, 15, 47, 83
Andrews, George, 27
Apollo 11, 11, 14, 47, 48, 52, 85
Apollo 12, 57, 58, 59
Apollo 14, 44, 59
Apollo 15, 56, 85, 86, 90
Apollo 17, 56
Apollo Expeditions to the Moon. *See* http://www.history.nasa.gov
Armstrong, Neeil, 47, 87
Armstrong, Neil, 12, 14
Artificial Moon Theory, 60

Assange, Julian, 37, 38
Astronautics Magazine, 60

B

Bean, Alan, 57
Blink 182. *See* Tom DeLonge
Brandenburg, Dr. John, 88
Brookings Institution, 34
Business Insider, 56

C

C.I.A., 74
Callimahos, Lambros D., 45
Campaigne, Dr. Howard H., 45
Capital Building, 71
Carey, Major General Michael, 43
Carlson, Gil, 38, 47, 83
Carpenter, Scott, 46
Catlin, James, 38
Centaur, 89
Cipher Bureau, 74, *See* NSA
Clementine Mission, 88
Clinton, Hillary Rodham, 40
Clinton, William Jefferson, (Bill), 39
Collins, Michael, 12, 14
Conrad, Pete, 57
Conway Daily Sun, 41
Cooper, William Milton (Bill), 74, 75, 76
Copernicus Crater, 70

Counter Intelligence Group, 32

D

Darwin, Charles, 52
Darwin, Sir George, 52
Darwin's Theory of Evolution. *See* Charles Darwin
Department of Defense, 34, 71, 84, 204
der Pol, Van, 66
Domes on the Moon, 68

E

Eagle, 12
Eisenhower, President Dwight David, 74, 75, 94
Extraterrestrial Intelligence (ETI), 44
EXTRA-TERRISTRAILS AMONG US. *See* George Andrews

F

formal treaty, 75
Freedom of Information Request, 33

G

Gagarin Crater, 62

H

Haut, Lieutenant Walter, 32
Hebrews Chapter 13, verse 2, 78
Hoagland, Richard, 69
Holloman Air Force Base, New Mexico, 76
Hosenball, S. Neil, 27

I

Irwin, James, 85

J

Jimmy Kimmel Live, 39, 41

K

Keel, John, 77
Kingu, 55
Kraft Jr., Christopher, 47

L

Linne, 65, 109
Lockheed Martin's Skunk Works, 43
LUNA 1, 12
LUNA 2, 12
Lunar Orbiter 2, 68
Lunar Prospector, 88

M

MacDoñald, Dr. Gordon, 60
man-made structures on the moon, 68
manned military outpost on the moon, 95
Mansfield, Terri, 44
MARA RABBI ALLARDI DINI ENDAVOUR ESA COUNS ALIM, 87
Marcel, Major Jesse, 31
Marcell, Jr, Jesse, 31
Marconi, Guglielmo, 67, 81
Mars, 69, 96
McCasland, Major General William, 43
McClelland, Clark, 90
Michael, Donald N., 34
Mission Control, 47, 84, 85, 86, 87
Mitchell, Edgar Dean (Ed), 44
Moon, 11, 12, 15, 22, 35, 46, 47, 50, 51, 52, 53, 54, 55, 58, 59, 60, 61, 62, 65, 66, 67, 68, 69, 70, 79, 81, 82, 83, 84, 86, 87,

88, 90, 93, 95, 96, 97, 99, 113, 160, 161, 164, 166, 170, 187, 195
moon rocks, 52

N

NASA, 11, 21, 24, 25, 27, 33, 34, 36, 44, 46, 47, 49, 60, 68, 69, 70, 84, 85, 87, 88, 89, 90, 95, 97, 99, 100, 104, 157, 164, 177, 185
NASA Administrator, 20, 26
NASA BOMBED THE MOON, 89
NASA Technical Report R-277, 99
NASA's Committee on Long Range Studies, 34
New Mexico, Corona, 31
New Mexico, Roswell, 16, 30, 31, 40, 74
NSA, 45, 74
NSA Technical Journal, Volume XI, No. 1, 45

O

O'Neill, John, 82
Obama, President Barack, 41, 42
Ohio University, 67
Our Haunted Planet. See Keel, John
Our Mysterious Spaceship Moon,. See Wilson, Don

P

Panama Canal Zone, 29, 30
Podesta, John, 41, 42, 44
Project CRYSTAL KNIGHT, 76
Project Horizon, 94, 95, 187
Project PLATO, 75
Project SIGMA, 74, 75
Proposed Studies on the Implications of Peaceful Space Activities for Human Affairs, 34

R

Ramey, General Roger M., 32
Ranger II, 68
Roswell Army Airfield, 31
ROSWELL Incident., 30

S

Schroeter, Johann. See Linne
See 509th Bomber Group".
Shcherbakov, Alexander, 60
Sitchin, Zecharia, 54
Sky and Telescope, 52
Sputnik 1, 33
Stormer, Carl, 66
Strategic Defense Initiative Organization, 88
Sumerian cosmology, 54, 55

T

Tesla, Nikola, 67
THE OCCULT CONNECTION, 4, 26
Third Reich, 14
Tiamat, 55
Title 14, Section 1211 of U.S. Federal Code, 20
Tom DeLonge, 42
Trudeau, Lieutenant General Arthur G., 94
Truly, Richard H., 28
Truman, President Harry S., 73
twelve-mile-long bridge, 82

U

UFO, 16, 17, 19, 26, 29, 30, 37, 39, 40, 42, 73
UFO Secrets Spilled by Wikileaks. See Carlson, Gil

United States Air Force Research Facility at Wright Patterson Air Force Base, 43

V

Valerian, Val, 76
Vasin, Michael, 60

W

Washington National Press Club, 69
water on the moon, 88
Watkins, Leslie, Alternative 3, 96
We were warned away, 87
Weiss, Rob, 43
White House, 40, 41, 42, 71
Wikileaks, 37, 38, 39
Wilson, Don, 60, 65, 67
Worden, Al, 86

www.ingramcontent.com/pod-product-compliance
Lightning Source LLC
Chambersburg PA
CBHW071912110526
44591CB00011B/1647